HE SPOKE TO THEM IN PARABLES

by

DR. DAVID EWERT

HE SPOKE TO THEM IN PARABLES

Copyright 2006, 2017

Published by HeartBeat Productions
Box 633
Abbotsford, BC
Canada V2S 6R7
email: heartbeatproductions@gmail.com

Scripture Quotations are taken from the New Revised Standard Version

All rights reserved. No portion of this book may be reproduced in any form without the written permission of the publisher.

Printed in USA

TABLE OF CONTENTS

Introduction 5

1. The Sower and the Seed (Mark 4:1-20) 11

2. The Waiting Father (Luke 15:11-32) 27

3. Surprised by Joy (Matthew 13:44-46) 43

4. The Good Samaritan (Luke 10:25-37) 55

5. The Unjust Steward (Luke 16: 1-13) 69

6. The Weeds Among the Wheat (Matthew 13:24-30; 36-43) .. 85

7. The Rich Man and Lazarus (Luke 16:19-3 1) 97

8. The Friend at Midnight (Luke 11:5-13) 115

9. The Pharisee and the Tax Collector (Luke 18:9-14) 125

10. The Mustard Seed and the Leaven (Matthew 13:32-33) .. 137

11. The Ten Maidens (Matthew 25:1-13) 147

12. The Sheep and the Goats (Matthew 25:31-46) 159

INTRODUCTION

There are few parts of the Bible so familiar to Bible readers as the parables of Jesus. Idioms derived from the parable stories of the Gospels have penetrated the English language. Even non-Christians, who do not read the New Testament parables, speak of being a good Samaritan, of passing by on the other side, of using or burying our talents, of counting the cost, of riotous living, of hiding one's lamp under a bushel, and so forth. All these and many other figures of speech have their origin in the parables of Jesus.

Although the parables are well known to Bible readers, it is hard to give a simple definition of a parable. They are, in one sense, extended similes. Many of them begin with the introductory formula: "The kingdom of heaven is like." When a younger child of Christian parents was asked on one occasion, which parts of the Bible she like most, she responded: "the like stories." Parables have sometimes been defined simply as "earthly stories with a heavenly meaning." A.M.Hunter in his book on parables (***The Parables Then and Now***) characterizes the parables in this rather interesting way: "A parable is one of those stories in the Bible which sounds at first like a pleasant yarn, but keeps something up its sleeve which suddenly pops up and leaves you flat." To be sure, Jesus' parables carry a powerful punch, but we must say a few more things about the meaning of "parable."

A. The Meaning of "Parable"

Our English word "parable" is derived directly from the Greek ***parabole*** According to its etymology the word means "to place alongside" for the purpose of comparison (***para***—beside; ***ballo***—to throw). It's a method of illustrating a truth (or truths). Newspapers often use cartoons. With a few simple lines the artist sketches a political, social, or economic message. Jesus did something similar with word pictures. The word ***parabole*** occurs fifty times in the New Testament. All but two of these occurrences are in the Synoptic Gospels (but see Heb 9:9 and 11:19). (The apostle John in his Gospel uses a synonym [***paroimia***] several times, although John has no parable stories, only parabolic sayings.)

However, behind the Greek language of the New Testament lies the Hebrew and Aramaic of the Gospel writers. And, as is the case with so many key Greek words of the New Testament, the word "parable" carries a Semitic meaning. Behind this Greek word lies the Hebrew ***mashal***, which has a much wider range of meaning than the Greek ***parabole***. It covers what we in English call parable, similitude, analogy, allegory, riddle, proverb, illustration, metaphor, or maxim. The parables of Jesus were first spoken orally in Aramaic, but they have come to us in Greek. Consequently the word "parable" must not be understood in a restricted sense, for it takes on the wider range of meaning from its Semitic background.

It is estimated that roughly one third of the recorded teachings of Jesus consist of parables or parabolic statements. Although only the Synoptic Gospels contain parable stories, the Gospel of John has a great many parabolic sayings. "Unless a grain of wheat falls into the ground and dies, it remains just a single seed; but if it dies, it bears much fruit" (Jn 12:24), is an example of a parabolic saying in the Fourth Gospel.

B. Characteristics of Parables

A parable is some common earthly thing, event, custom, or occurrence which Jesus used to illustrate some aspect of the kingdom of God. He takes his illustrations from everyday life—farming, marriage, family, household, business, and so forth, such as were familiar to his many audiences. A seed growing in the ground, a woman using yeast to bake bread, a sheep wandering away from the flock, and the like, were common everyday occurrences in the Palestine of Jesus' day.

The parable stories were designed to teach different aspects of the kingdom of God which Jesus had come to establish. They are not simple moralisms, not just good advice for daily living, not merely illustrations thrown into his discourses to make them more interesting. Jesus' parables illustrated how people might enter the kingdom of God, and how kingdom people ought to live. His eschatological parables even enlightened his hearers on the future dimension of the kingdom of God. Teaching by means of parables was not unique to Jesus. It was a well-known rabbinic method of instruction. Jesus spoke in parables in order to let the light of the gospel of the kingdom to shine into people's hearts. At the same time, they challenged his listeners to think and to make their own application. Some parables begin with "what do you think?" or end with "let him who has ears, hear (i.e., understand)."

Rarely did Jesus have to interpret the parables for his audiences (although there are several parables which Jesus expanded when he was alone with his disciples). Fee and Lewis, in their book, ***How to Read the Bible for All its Worth***, have a chapter on the interpretation of the parables. In it they point out, that for Jesus to interpret his parables would be like interpreting a joke, when the listener fails to get the point. What makes it funny is that the hearer catches it immediately. Once you try to explain it, it loses its force.

A few parables resemble allegories (e.g., The Parable of the Wheat and the Weeds), in which the details of the story are given meanings. Normally a parable has one basic thrust, and the details of the story are simply backcloth, staging, scenery, which gives context to the fundamental truth which Jesus is seeking to drive home. Since allegory became such a popular method of interpreting the Bible in the early centuries of the church, critical scholars today often take the position, that the allegorical elements of our Gospel parables do not go back to Jesus, but are the creation of the early church. However, there is no convincing reason why Jesus could not have availed himself of this method occasionally. Although we should avoid interpreting Jesus' parables allegorically, we should not object to the allegorical elements found in our Gospel parables. That allegory can also be a means of communicating biblical truth, can be seen clearly from the greatest allegory in the English language, John Bunyan's ***Pilgrim's Progress***, illustrating a Christian's journey through life, culminating in the eternal city. And that leads us to add a few more comments on the interpretation of parables.

C. The Interpretation of the Parables

In the early centuries of the Christian church two schools of interpretation were developed. The Alexandrian school preferred to interpret the Scriptures, and particularly the parables, allegorically. For example, in The Parable of the Good Samaritan, every item or individual mentioned in the story was given some meaning, often bordering on the bizarre. By contrast, the Antiochian school of interpretation was more wary and reserved when it came to allegory. As it happened, the allegorical method tended to dominate biblical exegesis throughout the Middle Ages.

The Protestant reformers broke with this popular method and encouraged a more literal and grammatical interpretation of the parables. Both Luther and Calvin used strong language in their denunciation of allegory, in which the interpreter's imagination often ran wild. At the end of the 19th century, Adolf Juelicher wrote two volumes on the parables of Jesus (***Die Gleichnisreden Jesu*** [vol. 1, 1888 vol 2, 1899]). He argued, that a parable has only one essential truth to teach, the details of the story do not need to be interpreted and shouldn't be, because such interpretations are usually quite arbitrary. Juelicher moved the study of the parables a step forward, but being a child of his times, and standing in a rather more liberal tradition, he often failed to find the main point of the parables.

The British New Testament scholar, C. H. Dodd, is credited with putting Jesus' parables into their proper theological context. In his ***Parables of the Kingdom*** (1935), he showed that our Gospel parables are all about the kingdom of God, and have to be interpreted from that vantage point. Where Dodd fell short was in his stress on what is called "realized eschatology." He stressed the presence of the kingdom in Jesus' ministry but evidently overlooked its future dimension, its glorious consummation. I. H. Marshall of Aberdeen, in a slender but important volume, ***Eschatology and the Parables*** (1963), showed that some of Jesus' parables clearly describe the end of the age, and not only the presence of the kingdom in the person of Jesus.

A German New Testament scholar, Joachim Jeremias, published a classic on the parables: ***Die Gleichhnisreden Jesus*** (1947, rev. 1963). He built on Dodd's foundation, although he would prefer to speak of "inaugurated eschatology." Since he grew up in Palestine, he was able to contribute important information on the cultural setting of the parables. Without some knowledge of the material, social, and religious culture of first century Palestine, the parables are much more difficult to understand. Jeremias has enriched this aspect of parable studies.

This is not the place to survey the mass of literature that has been published on the parables, but as long as God's people are serious about understanding the teachings of Jesus, new books on the parables will be written. In the following chapters I have chosen a number of parables stories and expounded them for Bible readers as well as for those who choose to preach from the parables. Younger students of Scripture often think that the parables are easier to interpret than, for example, the epistolary literature of the New Testament. The fact is, that parables are among the more difficult parts of Jesus' teachings to understand and to expound. If this volume should prove to be helpful in communicating the messages of the parables of Jesus, I would be grateful to God.

David Ewert, Professor of Biblical Studies, Emeritus,
Canadian Mennonite University, Winnipeg, Manitoba

CHAPTER ONE

THE SOWER AND THE SEED Mark 4:1-20

This woodcut is by an anonymous artist from Christoph Wiegel's **Biblia Ectypa: Bildnesse auss Heiliger Schrift, Alt und Neuen Testament** published in 1695.

In our study of the parables we want to focus on parable stories, rather than on the many brief parabolic utterances of Jesus found throughout the Gospels. Parable stories are what we might call extended similes. Although parables, as a rule, have one major thrust, they may also teach more than one subordinate truth about the kingdom of God. And that appears to be the case in the parable of the sower and the seed—a parable found in all three Synoptic Gospels (see Mt 13:1-9; Lk 8:4-8).

Jesus is at the seashore and crowds have gathered to hear him teach. According to Mark he had taught huge crowds beside Lake Galilee once before (see Mk 3:7). And just as on that occasion, so also this time round, Jesus sat down in a boat and taught the crowd on the shore. Jesus was at the zenith of his ministry when he spoke this parable; masses of people were coming to listen to him. However, he never manifested the triumphalism that often characterizes popular speakers. He knew that resistance to his message was building up, as the conclusion of Mark 3 clearly illustrates.

In both Mark and Matthew this parable has come to us in three clearly defined parts. First we have the parable of the four soils (Mk 4:3-9); this is followed by a rather enigmatic paragraph on the reason for speaking in parables (vv. 10-12). Finally, Jesus gives us an interpretation of the parable—something that is rather rare and unique. As a rule the curtain simply drops after Jesus has completed the parable story, and the audience must then make its own application, but not in this case.

Let us begin by focusing on the parable itself!

1. THE PARABLE OF THE SOWER AND THE SEED (Mk 4:3-9)

The parable begins with a call to "listen" (v. 3). That's how the Jewish confession of faith (the **Shema'**), recited daily by adult Jews, began. It's a summons to attentive hearing. Not only does the parable begin with a call to hear, but it also closes with the challenge, "let anyone with ears to hear, listen." The call to listen was not simply a rhetorical device to calm down the multitudes, it was a call that demanded also an obedient response to the word of God. The call to listen is followed by a call to "see." "Behold, a sower went out to sow" (v. 3). And this typical Galilean sower sows on different kinds of soil. The first kind mentioned is the hard ground.

A. The Hard Soil (vv. 3,4)

"Listen! A sower went out to sow. And as he sowed, some seed fell on the path, and the birds came and ate it up."

This parable reflects the agricultural practices of the Palestinian countryside in the days of Jesus. If the people on the seashore were not farmers themselves, they had all seen farmers seed their acreages. We must not judge the sower by modern farming methods. They had no seed drills in those days. Sowing was done by hand. Moreover, the sowing was done before spring plowing, and that explains why the seed lay exposed on the paths, inviting the birds to come and pick some of it up.

We have an illustration of this seeding pattern in the **Book of Jubilees** (11:11), a Jewish book from the intertestamental period: "And prince Mastema [i.e., the devil] sent ravens and birds to devour the seed which was sown in the land, in order to destroy the land and rob the children of men of their labors. Before they could plow in the seed, the ravens picked it from the surface of the ground."

We might wonder why the sower was so careless and sowed his seed even on the foot paths, where it was clearly visible to the birds, who came and fed on the seeds. But the path probably was one on which the villagers had walked in the course of the winter, when the fields lay fallow. A German commentator calls them ***Trampelpfade*** (trample paths). However, these may also have been the paths on the edges of the field. Fields were small in those days and normally not fenced in. And so as the sower scattered the seed on his acreage, some of it fell on the paths, where the birds came and picked it up.

B. The Rocky Soil (vv. 5,6)

"Other seed fell on rocky ground, where it did not have much soil, and it sprang up quickly, since it had no depth of soil. And when the sun rose, it was scorched, and since it did not have root, it withered away."

Again we might ask, why did this farmer sow his seed among the rocks? I grew up on a farm and one of the more detestable jobs was rock-picking—a job my father at times planned appropriately for Saturday, when we would be home from school. But again it is not fair to criticize this farmer for his agricultural practices. In fact sowing on rocky ground had little to do with his failure to clear the land of stones.

In Palestine a thin layer of soil often covers a limestone base, which is not visible to the eye. Once plowing will take place, the farmer will notice that parts of his acre have very shallow ground. In this kind of soil the seed germinates quickly, but because it has no roots, the plants wither and die, and there is no harvest.

Whether Jesus had a field in mind in which these different kinds of soil were present, or whether he was thinking of four different kinds of fields, is not clear. It doesn't affect the message or the meaning of the parable.

C. The Thorny Soil (v. 7)

"Other seed fell among the thorns, and the thorns grew up and choked it, and it yielded no grain."

There was next to no weed control in Jesus' day, and herbicides were unknown. Summer fallowing, as practised today, was also not known as a method of weed control. In fall, when the grain was cut, the weeds were cut together with the grain. They were then separated and the dried weeds were used for fuel. Then in spring, the farmer scattered his seed over his field once again, usually with a bag slung over his left shoulder. But the weeds got a head start, and eventually they choked the wheat before it was in head, and again there was no good yield of grain.

D. The Good Soil (v. 8)

"Other seed fell into good soil and brought forth grain, growing up and increasing and yielding thirty and sixty and hundredfold."

The good soil in this parable seems to bear an unusually high amount of grain. For a Palestinian farmer, some historians want to tell us, thirty-fold was considered to be a high yield. And it may be that Jesus wanted to suggest, that although much seed was lost on the poorer soil, there was still a rich harvest.

We should not try to read special meanings into the thirty, sixty, and hundredfold, as did some of the early Church Fathers. Cyprian, for example, thought those who bore hundredfold were the martyrs; the sixtyfold people were the celibates; and the thirtyfold represented the ordinary Christians. This was completely arbitrary and added nothing to the understanding of the parable's meaning.

The parable illustrates how differently people respond to the message of the kingdom. Jesus rounds off the parable with an exhortation to reflect on what he has said (v. 9). Obviously there was more to this parable than what appears on the surface. Later, when Jesus was alone with his disciples, and he gave them an interpretation of the parable, he expands its application.

When Jesus had finished the parable of the sower and the seed, his disciples came to him, asking why he used parables when he spoke to the people. And that leads us to consider what he had to say about the purpose of the parables.

II. THE PURPOSE OF THE PARABLES (vv. 10-13)

"When he was alone, those who were around him along with the twelve, asked him about the parables. And he said to them, To you has been given the secret of the kingdom of God, but for those outside, everything comes in parables, in order that they may indeed look, but not perceive, and may indeed listen, but not understand; so that they may not turn again and be forgiven."

From our first reading of this passage we get the impression, that Jesus spoke in parables in order to hide the message about the kingdom of God. But that can hardly have been Jesus' purpose. When we look at verses 33 and 34 we seem to get the opposite impression. "With many such parables he spoke the word to them, as they were able to hear it; he did not speak to them except in parables, but he explained everything in private." From these observations it seems rather clear, that Jesus did not tell parables in order to hide the truth from people. Rather, he adapted his parables to his audience, so that they would catch at least some glimpses of divine truth.

Returning now to verse 11, let us see how these strange words of Jesus can be understood! Jesus is responding to the question, why he spoke in parables. And he begins by telling his disciples, that to them had been given the secret of the kingdom of God. The passive of "given" is here used to say that God had given it to them. Jews did not want to use the name of God overly much, and so the passive voice was used. It is called the "divine passive." In other words, God had given the disciples of Jesus the ability to grasp something of the mystery of the kingdom of God. The Greek word *musteron* (mystery) is often used in the New Testament for divine revelation. It is called a mystery because God's plans of salvation are hidden from humans until he makes them known. A mystery is something hidden in God, but now made manifest in Jesus Christ. The disciples had grasped, at least in measure, the significance of the message of Jesus about God's kingdom, the reign he was establishing over the hearts and lives of people.

"But to those outside [i.e., the unbelievers], everything comes in parables." Here we must recall that behind the Greek word *parabole*, lies the Hebrew *mashal*, which covers a wide range of meanings, including that of "puzzle." In other words, unbelievers who refuse to open their hearts to the message of Jesus, are puzzled by his message. They hear the same words as those who embrace Jesus' message (i.e., the insiders), but his message seems enigmatic and they are puzzled by it; it remains a riddle to them. One is reminded of what Paul says in 1 Corinthians 1:14: "The person without the Spirit does not accept the things that come from the Spirit of God, but considers them foolishness, and cannot understand them because they are discerned only through the Spirit" (TNIV).

Jesus then reminds his disciples of a passage in Isaiah 6, in which the prophet, so it seems, looks back over his ministry, and in light of the strong resistance to his message, which he has had to endure, he sees himself as having been called to harden people's hearts.

The quotation from Isaiah 6:9,10 which the evangelist Mark (and Matthew) inserts between the telling of the parable of the sower and its interpretation, has been understood in the present context in different ways. There are critical scholars who argue that Jesus never quoted these words from Isaiah, but that the later church, when it saw that the Jews by and large, in contrast to Gentiles, were rejecting the gospel, attached

Isaiah's complaint to Jesus' teaching in parables. Mark then, they argue, simply took the church's explanation of Jewish resistance, and put these prophetic words into the mouth of Jesus. But that line of thinking leads us in the wrong direction, and is not worthy of our Gospel writers. There is no reason why Jesus should not have quoted these words from Isaiah 6 and applied them to his ministry. But what do they mean? Let me mention some attempts to understand these prophetic words!

(a) Mark introduces the quotation with the Greek ***hina.***, which ordinarily expresses purpose: "In order that." In other words, the purpose of the parables was to harden the hearts of unbelievers. But, as we have already mentioned (and this is borne out in v. 33), Jesus did not teach in parables so that the eyes of unbelievers would be blinded and their understanding darkened. That his message had this negative affect on some of his hearers, can, however, not be denied.

(b) Others suggest that ***hina*** need not necessarily express purpose all the time, and that the word should be read causally. In other words, "because they look but don't perceive, and listen but don't understand" they are not converted and their sins are not forgiven. In the parallel passage in Matthew 12:31, the Evangelist has the word "because" (***hoti***) instead of "in order that."

(c) Some understand ***hina*** in light of its Semitic background, as introducing a relative clause. "Who indeed look, but do not perceive," etc., and consequently are not converted.

(d) The word ***hina*** upon occasion introduces a result rather than a purpose clause. The line between purpose and result is often quite thin. Some English versions, in fact, introduce the quotation from Isaiah with "so that." In other words, Jesus is making an observation on how people who reject his message experience the darkening of their understanding and consequently refuse to return to God.

(e) Another suggestion is that ***hina*** is shorthand

for "in order that it may be fulfilled." In other words, what happened in the days of the prophet Isaiah was being repeated in the days of our Lord. Just as Israel had rejected the prophet's message, so people in Jesus' audience were rejecting his message, and did not turn to God to receive forgiveness for their sins. But whether we read **hina** as shorthand or not, Jesus does seem to be saying, that what happened in the days of Isaiah, when people heard God's message but hardened their hearts, is being repeated in his own ministry. "Seeing they see, but do not perceive; hearing they hear, but do not understand, and so they don't turn around and find forgiveness for their sins." It was not Jesus' intention to blind eyes or darken understanding; he wanted to win people for the kingdom of God by using parables. But when people refused to accept his message, that same word of God hardened their hearts. "Light accepted leads to light; light rejected leads to night."

And with that perspective we go back to the parable of the sower. The disciples had asked Jesus for a better understanding of this parable (v. 13), and Jesus seemed a bit puzzled, that they had not grasped the full import of his message. But, as verse 34 suggests, "He did not speak to them except in parables, but he explained everything in private to his disciples." In the verses 13-20 Jesus patiently draws out the meaning of the parable. Perhaps it would be more correct to speak of this interpretation as a practical application of the parable.

III. THE INTERPRETATION OF THE PARABLE (vv. 13-20)

Verse 13 is a transitional statement. The disciples must have asked Jesus for a more explicit interpretation of the parable of the sower, and Jesus responds with a question (or is it a statement?) which expresses a bit of surprise at the lack of spiritual acumen on the part of his disciples. "Do you not understand this parable? Then how will you understand all the parables?" The singular "parable" in the first part of Jesus' comment, ties this expansion of the parable closely to the parable as told in the verses 3-12. It has often been observed by Bible readers that of all our Gospel writers, no one underscores the weaknesses of the disciples as much as Mark. Again and again he observes that they were lacking in spiritual perception and in faith. Jesus rebukes them occasionally, but he will not let them go. He wants to mold them into solid pillars on which he will build his church.

Many critical scholars are of the opinion, that the parable itself represents an authentic parable story as told by Jesus, but that the interpretation that now follows comes from the later church and is being read back into the mouth of Jesus. Without rehearsing the arguments for such a viewpoint, I would suggest, that there is no convincing reason why this interpretation of the parable should not also have come from Jesus himself.

Verse 14 is introductory. "The sower sows the word." Clearly then, Jesus is using the verb to "sow" in a figurative sense. Whether this typical sower was sowing wheat or barley seed is of no consequence. He is sowing God's word. Paul later speaks of sowing spiritual good in the lives of the Corinthians, when he proclaimed the good news to them (1 Cor 9:11). Although Mark does not identify the sower, it is clear from the context that in the first instance Jesus is meant. That does not limit the application, however, for all those who proclaim and witness to the word of God are also sowers of the word. And "word" does not have to be explained, for when Mark wrote his Gospel, the readers already knew, that it was the good news of the kingdom of God that Jesus had in mind.

Jesus was proclaiming the message of the kingdom of God, a message which offered forgiveness of sins, and the gift of eternal life to all those who believed and became members of God's kingdom. With verse 15 we seem to have a slight shift, for now the seed that is sown are people. And people respond in different ways to the word of God. Perhaps it would be best if we thought of the seed that is sown as having a double meaning; first, it is the word of God that is sown, and then it is also the people who hear the word and respond to it in different ways.

A. Those Upon the Path (v. 15)

"These are the ones on the path where the word is sown: when they hear, Satan immediately comes and takes away the word that is sown in them."

Although Jesus is not excusing those who reject the word, or absolving them of personal responsibility, he acknowledges the power of the evil one to destroy the work of God in the hearts of those who hear the gospel. Satan puts up fierce resistance to the message of the kingdom, and does everything within his power to neutralize the effect of God's word on those who hear it.

We should always understand the teachings of Jesus in their original setting, but we must not leave them in the first century. It is the task of the expositor of scripture to show the significance of Jesus' teachings for our day. The devil's tactics, of course, have not changed, and just as in Jesus' day, so in our day he is bent on taking away the word sown in the hearts of men and women. We should not try to be wiser than Jesus and relegate the concept of Satan to the dark ages; Satan is very much alive and active today and seeks to destroy God's work wherever he can.

Satan attacks people in a great variety of ways. The first time we meet the evil one in the pages of scripture is in the garden of Eden (Gen 3:1-3), where, in the form of a serpent, he puts doubts about the word of God into the minds of our first parents. And, after putting God's word in doubt, he flatly contradicts it (Gen 3:4). But there are numerous other ways in which Satan seeks to undermine and annul the word of

God. In the Lucan parallel we read, "Then the devil comes and takes away the word from their hearts, that they may not believe and be saved" (8:12). The hearing of God's word, attended by faith, is God's means of salvation.

B. Those on Rocky Ground (vv. 16,17)

"And these are the ones sown on rocky ground: when they hear the word, they immediately receive it with joy. But they have no root, and endure only for a while; then when trouble or persecution arises on account of the word, immediately they fall away."

Here we have a situation in which people embrace the message of the kingdom with joy, but they are "ephemeral" (The Greek *proskairos* means temporal, for the moment, short-lived.) Because their faith has only shallow roots, they apostatize when they encounter difficulties because of the gospel of the kingdom, the "word." Jesus is quite realistic. He expects his followers to be subjected to persecution, and they will have to endure tribulation from time to time. Tribulation is a more general word for the difficulties that believers can expect to face because they are kingdom people; persecution is the more specific word. It should be noted that Jesus is not speaking of weak or fickle characters, but of believers who are attacked from "the outside."

It may seem strange that the message of the kingdom, which offers forgiveness of sins and the hope of eternal life, should become the occasion for persecution. But those who become members of Christ's kingdom, have pledged their supreme loyalty to Christ as their Lord. They seek to live godly lives, and that makes them a kind of "contrast society," provoking unbelievers (although not deliberately) to harass and persecute Christ's followers.

"Immediately they fall away." To fall away is English for one Greek word: *skandalizomai* (from which our word "scandal" is derived). It means to stumble and to fall. They abandon the faith. Some of the fiercest antagonists of the Christian faith are people who at one time in their life accepted the gospel and then apostatized. Chuck Tempelton, journalist and editor, was in his earlier years an evangelist and an associate of Billy Graham. But he abandoned the Christian faith and wrote a book entitled **Farewell to God**. How sad!

C. Those Among the Thorns (vv. 18,19)

"And others are those sown among the thorns: these are the ones who hear the word, but the cares of the world, and the lure of wealth, and the desires for other things come in and choke the word, and it yields nothing."

Although it is not stated explicitly that these people receive the word with joy, as was the case with the previous group, that must be assumed. To "hear the word" often means more than just listening to the gospel, for the word "hear" can also mean to obey the message. (In German we distinguish between ***horchen*** and ***gehorchen***—to hear and to obey—although both words have to do with hearing.) Of those sown on the rocky ground it is said, that they fall away and give up the faith. That is also not stated here. However, when it is said that the thorns among which these people are sown, "choke the word, and it proves unfruitful," the meaning is not too different. In their case the seed simply does not survive.

Whereas the previous group abandoned the faith because of persecution, these sown on rocky ground are tempted to fall away for different reasons. The cares of this present age, the worries about the present life, weigh so heavily upon them, that the seed that was sown is choked. Added to the worries of the present life, Jesus mentions the "lure of wealth." The Greek word ***apate*** can indeed mean lure or delight, but it has another meaning as well, and that is "deceit." Luke in his parallel account has "the lust for life" (8:14—***hedone*** in Greek gives us the English "hedonism"). Robert Mounce, in his commentary on Matthew, writes: "To be caught up in the worries of everyday living and to fall prey to the seductive appeal of financial well-being is to guarantee a spiritual crop failure."

Interestingly Jesus does not mention doubts or intellectual difficulties as reasons for falling away. These are often given as the reasons for abandoning the Christian faith, but sometimes they serve as a smoke screen to cover up a person's unwillingness to obey the ethical demands of the gospel.

Besides the worries about everyday life in the present age, and the lure (or the deceitfulness) of riches, which choke the seed of the word, Mark concludes with a comprehensive statement: "and all the other desires that enter into people that choke the word, and it proves unfruitful." Professor Helmut Thielicke, in his book on parables (***Das Bilderbuch der Bibel***), says of this parable: "I wonder whether we have caught the sadness that hangs over this story? The parable is really pointing out how frequently the divine seed is destroyed—destroyed in stony hearts, by the heat of the sun, by choking thorns and predatory birds—this is why there is in this parable a deep sense of grief and sorrow." Fortunately, however, that is not all there is in this parable. There is another kind of hearer who is mentioned last, who hears the word and bears rich fruit.

D. Those On Good Soil (v. 20)

"And these are the ones sown on the good soil: they hear the word and accept it and bear fruit, thirty and sixty and hundredfold."

Here it is explicitly stated that those sown on good soil heard the word of God and embraced it, welcomed it (Matthew in the parallel has "understand" it; Luke has "they hold it fast"). And the result of such a reception of the word, in which the seed, with all its theological and ethical implications, sinks deep into the heart, is that it yields a rich harvest. Thirtyfold, sixtyfold, and a hundredfold means that the good soil produced thirty, sixty, and a hundred times as much as was sown. One is reminded of Paul's saying in Galatians 6:8, "if you sow to your own flesh, you will reap corruption from the flesh; but if you sow to the Spirit, you will reap eternal life from the Spirit."

In conclusion it should be pointed out, that we must not see in these different responses to the word of God, four classes of people. That would lead to determinism and would undermine the human responsibility to respond to the gospel. We must not say, that this or that person is by constitution a shallow person, or that someone is genetically so programmed that he or she will take a greater interest in material things. Nor should we compare someone to a weather vane that turns with the wind. But neither can we say that some people are by bent of their personality devout, religious or godly. The fact is, that every individual has all four kinds of soil within him or herself

Today Jesus is addressing us as he addressed the crowds in his day, and he is warning us, not to be like the seed that fell on the path, or on the shallow ground, or among the thorns. He is exhorting us, as he did when he spoke to the crowds by the lakeside, to receive the word of God joyfully with open hearts and let it bear fruit in our lives. The apostle James encourages his readers to "welcome with meekness the implanted word that has the power to save [our] souls" (1:21).

CHAPTER TWO

THE WAITING FATHER Luke 15:11-32

This woodcut is by an anonymous artist from Christoph Wiegel's **Biblia Ectypa: Bildnesse auss Heiliger Schrift, Alt und Neuen Testament** published in 1695.

THE WAITING FATHER Luke 15:11-32

A variety of titles has been given to this parable—one of the best known of all the parables of Jesus: "The Parable of the Prodigal Son," "The Parable of Two Prodigal Sons," "The Parable of the Lost Son," "A Parable of a Dysfunctional Family," and so forth. I have chosen the title: "The Waiting Father"—a title suggested by the German theologian, Helmut Thielicke, in his book on parables. This parable is unique in the sense that only Luke records it.

Actually the parable of the waiting father is one of a trilogy of parables found in Luke 15, and all three appear to be a defense of Jesus' redemptive and compassionate mission. Scribes and Pharisees criticize Jesus for welcoming sinners and having fellowship with them. The introduction (vv. 1-3) depicts a situation in which tax collectors and sinners are anxious to listen to Jesus' teachings. They were open to the message of Jesus about the kingdom of God, although there is no explicit reference in this chapter to the kingdom. Tax collectors were a despised lot, for they worked hand in glove with the Roman overlords, and were known for lining their own pockets by overcharging people. Although tax collectors would also be seen by Jewish society as sinners, in this context the word "sinners" seems to be used of a group other than tax collectors. Very likely it's a reference to those people who did not conform to the holiness code of the temple.

The Pharisees and the scribes were offended when Jesus taught such a despicable lot, and, to top it off, he even ate with them. Eating was regarded as worse than mere association; it implied welcome and recognition. But Jesus would not allow the criticism of the religious authorities to interfere with his ministry of calling sinners to repentance. The Pharisees, of course, would not share table fellowship with people whom they regarded as sinful, and so they grumble (***diagonguzo*** is a verb in which the sound and the sense agree, as in murmur, or grumble). In response to their critical attitude, Jesus tells three parables. All three stress the joy of finding what was lost—the sheep, the coin, and the son. The last of the three parables, however, is drawn out in much greater detail than the first two, and it is on the parable of the waiting father that we want to focus—a parable that many scholars regard as the finest of all the parables of Jesus. This parable actually has two parts to it: not only will the family rejoice when the lost son returns home, but the elder brother like the Pharisees, will refuse to enter into this joy.

I. THE LOST SON (vv. 11-24)

A. The Demand (vv. 11,12)

"Then Jesus said, There was a man who had two sons. The younger of them said to the father, 'Father, give me the share of the property that will belong to me'."

Most of the parable is devoted to the younger of the two sons. It is not until we come to verse 25 that we meet the elder son. The younger son may have been no more than seventeen, for evidently he was not yet married. In ancient Israel young men, as a rule, married between 18 and 20, although not always.

According to Old Testament law (Deut 21:17), the elder son was entitled to a double share of the property. In that case the younger son would have been eligible for one third of the family estate. However, if the disposition of the property was made before the death of the father, the sons would get less, for the father would not deprive himself of all means of livelihood. In the **Wisdom of Sirach** fathers are warned not give over their property to their sons while they (i.e., the fathers) are still living (Eccles. 33:18-21) Moreover, there were, as a rule, restrictions on what the sons were allowed to do with their inherited property as long as the father lived.

In this parable the younger son demands, and obtains, his share of the family estate, as well as the right to dispose of the property. The elder son no doubt also got his share when the father divided his property between his two sons. And that may explain the remark in verse 31, "All that is mine is yours." For a son to demand his share of the inheritance before the father died was synonymous with saying, "Father, I am eager for you to die." And if this father had been like other fathers in his day, he might have driven his son from home. But, as the parable will show, he is quite unlike most fathers.

If we ask, what the inheritance may have consisted of, the answer would be clothes, and land, and cattle. This father must have been a man of means, for he had servants, and his house had a banquet hall in which a crowd of neighbors later could gather and have a party. The fact that the neighbors were happy to accept the invitation to celebrate, indicates the respect the father had in the village.

By demanding that the father divide up his property, this son violated his filial relationship with his father. His language betrays his bad attitude:

"Give me the part that belongs to me." Nothing destroys human relations, including marriages, so often as selfish demands. Evidently this young scoundrel wanted to be independent, free, forgetting, that to be a child of the father is the greatest freedom. But that's a lesson he will learn the hard way in the far off country.

B. The Departure (v. 13)

"A few days later the younger son gathered all he had and traveled to a distant country, and there he squandered his property in dissolute living."

Apparently the son was in a hurry to get away from

his family, for he left "a few days later." Perhaps he was anxious to leave his village after it became public how shamefully he had treated his father. The son leaves and the wordless father watches him as he disappears in the distance. "The father couldn't compel his son to stay home. He couldn't force his love on the beloved. He had to let him go in freedom, even though he knew the pain it would cause both his son and himself" (Henry Nouwen, ***The Return of the Prodigal***).

A vast number of Jews in those days left their homeland and traveled to the bigger cities to make money. Many times more Jews lived in the Diaspora than in Palestine in Jesus' day. This young man, however, had not yet learned how to make money or how to handle it. He was out to have a good time.

There is something terribly callous about the son's behavior. But the father never says a word. We can only imagine what went on in his mind. Will he ever come back? How will he come back? How will the villagers react if he comes back? In those days it mattered to the whole village what individual members of the community did. The entire village would have been deeply disturbed by what the younger son did. Family solidarity was considered essential for the survival of peasant society. The younger son had failed the entire community.

If we ask, how could he "gather together" all that the father had given him? the answer may lie in one of the meanings of the Greek verb ***sunago***. Normally it means, quite literally, "to gather together." However, there is another meaning, found in the New English Bible: "he turned everything into cash." If he hadn't done this, he would not have been able to travel to a distant country so easily.

And, having arrived at his destination, "he squandered his property in dissolute living." No doubt, with pockets full of money, he soon had friends. He ate well and lived in grand style. Whether he also engaged in sexual immorality is not stated explicitly, although his older brother later accused him, rightly or wrongly, of prostitution (v. 30). All we know is, that he lived recklessly, dissolutely, in a debauched and profligate manner. And it wasn't long before he ran out of money.

C. The Distress (vv. 14-16)

"When he had spent everything, a severe famine took place throughout the country, and he began to be in need. So he went and hired himself out to one of the citizens of that country, who sent him to his fields to feed the pigs. He would gladly have filled himself with the pods that the pigs were eating; and no one gave him anything."

To begin with he had plenty of money. But money alone does not fill the void in people's lives, and so he indulged in the pleasures of the flesh. People around him may have looked with envy upon this dashing spendthrift. Perhaps they saw in him an example of the good life. Of course, they could not see through the facade behind which guilt, frustration and boredom lurked. But with no father to guide him, he spent his money in reckless abandon. Then a famine broke out and reality began to hit home. He began to suffer need. He could have gone home, but he had broken all the rules of family and community life, and would not be welcome. So he must try to get a job.

He "attached" himself to one of the citizens of that country. The verb may suggest that the man didn't really want him. His would-be employer was obviously a Gentile, for he kept pigs. There is a Jewish saying, that has it, "Cursed is he who feeds pigs." Jews were forbidden to raise hogs, since the eating of pork was forbidden. Feeding pigs was about as low as a Jew could sink. And what was even worse: he desired to fill himself with the pods which the pigs ate, but no one gave him anything. It looks as if the owner of these pigs did not even allow him to eat the pods which the pigs ate. Joachim Jeremias suggests, that either he had to keep alive by stealing food or else his employer gave him very meagre rations, but not the pods which the pigs ate. Carob pods were used as fodder, and only the very poor ever ate them. A Jewish rabbi wrote, "When Israelites are reduced to carob pods, then they repent." Helmut Thielicke imagines this lost son saying to himself, "I wanted to become myself, and thought I would get all this by cutting myself off from my father and my roots, fool that I am. I have found nothing but chains—and a bitter laughter goes up from the pigsty."

D. The Despair (vv. 17-19)

"But when he came to himself he said, 'How many of my father's hired hands have bread enough and to spare, but here I am dying of hunger! I will get up and go to my father, and I will say to him, Father, I have sinned against heaven and before you. I am no longer worthy to be called your son; treat me as one of your hired hands'."

"When he came to himself' is understood by some Bible readers to mean simply that this wastrel finally got smart. I. H. Marshall, however, suggests that it is a Semitic way of expressing repentance. William Barclay makes the observation that this was the highest compliment our Lord ever paid a human being. In effect, Jesus is saying, that when people are far from God, they are not their true selves. It is, of course true, that we were created for God, and so much of our misery stems from not being what we were made to be. To be in fellowship with God is to be authentically human.

The young man is at his wits end; he is in despair. Despair can also lead to nihilism and sometimes to suicide. Despair alone never leads people back to the Father's house. However, in this case, repentance was born out of despair. His memory of his father's house led him to repent. "Feelings lie buried that grace can restore," says the songwriter. His was a grief unto life, and not unto death (2 Cor. 7:10). Repentance gives human beings true dignity, for in repentance they assume responsibility for their deeds or misdeeds. To accept responsibility goes a long way in the process of restoration to fellowship with the father. A thief who was serving time in prison was asked, "Was it worth it?" "Worth it?" he replied. "I can't help it." In other words, he would not accept responsibility for his thievery. But the young man in our parable accepts responsibility for his misery and decides to return to his father

Kenneth Bailey in his book on parables warns us not to make a Pelagian out of this young man, by giving him credit for taking the initiative in his decision to turn his life around. In fact he suggests that this young man was devising a clever scheme of becoming a hired servant of his father, recouping his losses, and in that way to become integrated into the family and the community once again. But that way of reading the text does not seem to be the majority opinion. Having come to himself, the young man decides to return to his father.

E. The Return (v. 20)

"So he set off and went to his father. But while he was still far off, his father saw him and was filled with compassion; he ran and put his arms around him and kissed him."

The lost son has decided to return not simply to his village or to his home, but to his "father." Now it is no longer hunger alone that drives him, although he was hungry to be sure. Nor is he driven by loneliness. He is driven by guilt. He has realized that he has sinned egregiously against a loving father. John Bunyan writes, that when his eyes were first opened to his own guilt, he would have run to the Father, even if the Father had met him with a dagger, for he could not longer bear his guilt.

The old gentleman must have hoped and watched for his son's return for a long time. And when his father saw him he ran to meet him. This was most unusual and was considered undignified for an older oriental man. No doubt he drew his long outer garment up around his waist and ran to welcome his wayward son. One writer suggests, that the father wanted to be the first to meet the boy, for if other villagers had seen him first, he might not have fared all that well at their hands.

And when his father saw him he had compassion on him. The verb "to have compassion" suggests that his "insides" (the upper viscera) were agitated (***splagchnizomai***). When the father met his lost son, he fell on his neck, i.e., he put his arms around him and kissed him. The compound verb "to kiss" (***kataphileo***) suggests that be kissed him repeatedly or, at least, he kissed him affectionately, tenderly. Nothing perfunctory about this greeting! The language is reminiscent of Genesis 33:4, where we read of Esau, that he "ran to him [Jacob] and fell on his neck and kissed him and wept." Kissing was a sign of forgiveness and the restoration of broken relationships.

They tell the story of an English country boy who had the chance to go to the city and to attend a cathedral service. The lesson that day happened to be the parable of the prodigal son. It was new to him, and he listened with eyes, ears and mouth. And when the reader of the story came to the words, "when the father saw him he had pity on him and ran and threw his arms around him and kissed him," he exploded in the words, "Eh, but that was a grand old man."

F. The Confession (v. 21)

"Then the son said to him, 'Father, I have sinned against heaven and before you; I am no longer worthy to be called your son'."

He confessed that he had sinned against "heaven." Heaven was a common substitute for God, since Jews did not want to use his holy name too frequently. "God is in heaven and you are on earth," said the rabbis, and so one should be careful how one addressed God. But the son had also sinned grievously against his father, his entire family, and against society. It is worth noting that when we sin against others, we are also sinning against God. David had sinned against Bathsheba and her husband Uriah, but when he made his confession he said, "against you alone have I sinned" (Ps 51:4).

He then told his father that he was no longer worthy to be his son. Actually he had planned to say even more. When he decided to return home, he wanted to ask his father to make him one of his hired servants. But he didn't get to that. Did his father not let him finish his intended confession? (Incidentally, some pedantic scribe did carry over from verse 19 all that the son intended to say, and it got into some manuscripts. But the shorter reading is preferred by textual scholars.)

The Scottish theologian, Thomas Smail, in his book, ***The Forgotten Father***, imagines the son rehearsing his confession before he met his father. "Make me as one of your hired servants. I can never expect to be in your dining room, drawing room... family circle again. Give me a little lean-to behind the cowshed—I will do every duty you prescribe and otherwise keep quiet and not draw attention to myself, provided you will put up with me." Smail then adds, that there are some orthodox Christians whose expectations of God are not much better than that.

The picture of a respected oriental father embracing and kissing his son who brought such shame on the house, is rather unique. One might have expected a mother to receive such a lost son in this manner, but not the father. A Sunday school teacher was telling this parable to children in a city slum area. And when she came up to this point in the story, she asked the children the question, "And what do you think the father did?" "Bash him," came the united response. F. F. Bruce writes (***The Message***), "His father might have said: "That's all very well young man; we have heard fine speeches before. Now you buckle to and work as you have said, and if it turns out that you meant what you say, we may let you work your passage. But first prove yourself we can't just let bygones be bygones as though nothing happened. Even that would have been generous; it might have done the young man a world of good, and the elder brother himself might have been content to let him be put on probation... But it was not Jesus' picture of God." The story begins with the son demanding, "Give me ...! And that led the son into ruin. But now the language has changed to "Forgive me!" and that led to restoration and wholeness.

G. The Restoration (vv. 22-24)

"But the father said to his slaves, 'Quickly, bring out a robe—the best one—and put it on him; put a ring on his finger and sandals on his feet. And get the fatted calf and kill it, and let us eat and celebrate; for this son of mine was dead and is alive again; he was lost and is found!' And they began to celebrate."

The father restores his son's honor and integrates him into the family once more. He gives him a robe—the best one at that. When a king wished to honor an official, he might give him a costly robe. Some scholars think there is an allusion in our text to Zechariah 3:4, where the angel of the Lord tells bystanders to take the filthy garment from Joshua, and then adds, "behold I have caused your iniquity to pass from you and I will clothe you with rich apparel." Certainly when God forgives a sinner he gives him back his self-respect.

To put a ring on his finger meant that he was given back his standing, his dignity in the family. When Joseph received a ring from Pharaoh it gave him status (Gen 41:42). Also, he is to have shoes on his feet. He probably came home barefoot. But to walk barefoot was a sign of slavery. Free men and women had shoes. "All o' God's children got shoes," sang the black slaves on the southern plantations.

But the highlight of the son's restoration was the

celebration that followed. The fatted calf the one kept for a special occasion, was to be slaughtered. Meat was not eaten every day in first century Palestine. But this was a banquet to which the neighbors were going to be invited. If the villagers ate together with the son who had returned, he would be reintegrated into the community. The chapter began with the observation that Jesus ate with sinners. Eating together meant to be in fellowship with one another. It was to be a happy occasion. "Let us celebrate," says the father. And the reason? His dead son was alive again, and the lost son had been found. These two metaphors are an example of synonymous parallelism. There follows then a ***symphonia*** (our word "symphony")—loud singing, hand clapping, dancing and skipping.

The story so far has given us a truly marvelous picture of who God is. There is no question about who the father in the parable represents; it is God. And the lost son obviously represents the tax-collectors and sinners, mentioned at the beginning of the chapter. In a masterful way Jesus forced his hearers to acknowledge that the father who took back his wayward son, did the right thing. Even the most hard-boiled hearer had to admire this father. And so our Lord has justified his salvatory mission. In effect Jesus is saying: If I receive sinners, I am doing what the father in this story did, and you know that's the way God acts.

But there is a sequel to this story of love and forgiveness. That part of the story will cast a searchlight on those who objected to the grace that Jesus was showing to the sinful and despised members of society.

II. THE ELDER BROTHER (vv. 25-32)

"Now the elder son was in the field, and when he came and approached the house, he heard music and dancing. He called one of the slaves and asked what was going on. He replied, 'Your brother has come and your father has killed the fatted calf, because he got him back safe and sound.' Then he became very angry and refused to go in. His father came out and began to plead with him. But he answered his father, 'Listen! For all these years 1 have been working like a slave for you, and I have never disobeyed your command; yet you have never given me even a young goat so that I might celebrate with my friends. But when this son of yours comes back, who has devoured your property with prostitutes, you killed the fatted calf for him!' Then the father said to him, 'Son, you are always with me, and all that is mine is yours. But we had to celebrate and rejoice, because this brother of yours was dead and has come to life; he was lost and he has been found'."

Up to this point in the parable the generous efforts of the father have succeeded in restoring the beleaguered family. The prodigal son has been reconciled to the father and the father and his son to the village. All appears to have gone well so far. But the elder brother's refusal to participate in the banquet was totally unexpected. It is shocking. The absence of the elder son at the banquet would be noticed immediately by the neighbors. It was not uncommon in that culture that the elder son would welcome the guests. With this elder son sulking outside, while the rest of the family celebrated, the neighbors could not help but think that this family was altogether dysfunctional.

Again the father takes the initiative. He goes out to the eldest son and begins to beg him to come in. The eldest son (in contrast to the lost son in verse 21) omits the respectful address. He accuses his father of being partial, unjust and unfair. Also, he cannot get himself to call the prodigal "brother." "When this one comes back," he says. He accuses his younger brother of wasting the family fortune. And finally he gets nasty: "He wasted your property with harlots." There is nothing in the story itself that indicates that, and it seems to be an attempt on the part of the elder brother to make the past of the prodigal blacker than it really was. In any case, he accuses his father of gross unfairness: "You have killed the fatted calf."

This is a remarkable scene. In the culture of the Near East fathers do not, as a rule, entreat their sons; they order them. To beg them, was thought to be demeaning. But the father in this parable has already acted out of character by running to embrace his lost son and restoring him to the family and the community. And now the father repeatedly (the verb ***parakaleo*** is in the imperfect) entreats his elder son to come and join in the celebration. And he addresses him kindly, using, what is called a caritative, in speaking to him. "Child," he says, "you are always with me and all that belongs to me is yours." "We had to rejoice and be glad." Implied is, of course, "and you should also rejoice."

And with that this two-pronged parable comes to an end. Jesus doesn't need to make any applications; the message is clear and powerful. We would love to know whether the elder son joined the party, whether the younger son made out well; how the family got along after all that had happened. But that may have blunted the message of the parable.

CONCLUSION

We should not expect a parable to teach us the many aspects of how one enters the kingdom of God. But the parable proclaims the love of God which seeks the lost and restores them to fellowship. It is a powerful commentary on the biblical doctrine of forgiveness. We should not infer from this parable that God takes sin lightly. Forgiveness is costly. Sinners who heard Jesus tell this story must have rejoiced that God's love encompassed them as well. The Pharisees, however, must have cringed, for they could not help but realize that Jesus was in effect doing what the father in the parable did. And they couldn't avoid seeing themselves mirrored in the grumbling of the elder brother, who couldn't rejoice at the return of his wayward brother. The spiritually dead were coming to life; the lost were returning to the father's house; and they stood outside like the elder brother, joyless, loveless, self-righteous, and closed to the good news of the kingdom. "Christ Jesus came into this world to save sinners" (I Tim 1:15).

CHAPTER THREE

SURPRISED BY JOY Matthew 13:44-46

This woodcut is by an anonymous artist from Caspar Luiken's **Historiae celebriores Veteris Testamenti Iconibus representatae** published in 1712.

SURPRISED BY JOY Matthew 13:44-46

Matthew has structured his Gospel in such **a** way, that narrative alternates with discourse. There are five major discourses in Matthew, and chapter 13 is the third. In this chapter the Evangelist has collected eight parables—all of them illustrating some aspect of the kingdom of the heavens. Several of these parables are found also either in Mark or in Luke, but the one we are about to focus on is found in Matthew only. It is a twin parable: the treasure in the field and the pearl of great value.

Both parables, in their own unique way, speak about the discovery of the kingdom of God. And both of them stress the joy of discovering it. In both cases, also, there is an element of surprise. And so it is quite fitting to borrow the title of C. S. Lewis's autobiography, ***Surprised by Joy***, as a caption for our reflections on these twin parables. They appear, at first, to be so simple and innocent, but they carry a powerful message. In effect they are telling us, that the kingdom of God is of greater value than anything else on this earth, and that everything must be sacrificed in order to attain it.

These parables, like all the parables of Jesus, were addressed to a Palestinian audience, and have to be understood in the context of first century Jewish culture. Also, we have to ask what these parables meant for the people who heard them for the first time. That question, however, has to be expanded, for we also need to hear what Christ is saying to us in the twenty-first century. A proper interpretation of these parables, then, will call for a combination of exegesis and of application.

Implied in these parables, when first spoken by Jesus, is the presence of the kingdom of heaven (or God). Secondly, these parables speak of the discovery of God's kingdom. And thirdly, the parables illustrate the supreme value of the kingdom that Jesus brought.

We want to approach these two very short parables from these three vantage points.

I. THE PRESENCE OF THE KINGDOM

"The kingdom of heaven is like treasure hidden in a field, which someone found and hid; then in his joy he goes and sells all that he has and buys that field. Again the kingdom of heaven is like a merchant in search of fine pearls; on finding one pearl of great value, he went and sold all that he had and bought it" (vv. 44-46).

When Jesus speaks of the kingdom of heaven, he is not using the word kingdom in a territorial or political sense, as, for example, in "The Kingdom of Jordan." Basically "kingdom" (***basileia*** in Greek) means kingly reign or rule. The kingdom of the heavens is God's sovereign reign, and this reign broke into this world with the coming of Jesus. God, of course, does not rule over a vacuum, but over the hearts and lives of people who acknowledge him as their Sovereign.

That was, however, not the way Jesus' Jewish audiences in the first century understood the concept of the kingdom of God. They were hoping that a prince from the house of David would arise, overthrow the Romans, and establish once again the kingdom of David. The Gentiles would be destroyed and the boundaries of the ancient Davidic kingdom would be restored. But that was not the purpose of Jesus' coming. When he was accused before Pilate of being a rival king, Jesus explained, that his kingdom was not of this world (Jn 18:36).

Jesus began his Galilean ministry with the message, "Repent for the kingdom of heaven has come near" (Mt 3:17). With the coming of Jesus, God was establishing his kingly reign over people, and those who repented and put their faith in Christ, were granted the privilege of becoming members of his kingdom. That the kingdom of God had become a present reality in Jesus could be seen, said Jesus, in his mighty deeds. "If I by the Spirit of God cast out demons, then the kingdom of God has come to you" (Lk 11:20). His reply to the doubting Baptist, who was languishing in prison, wondering whether Jesus was the Messiah, was this: the blind see, the lame walk, the dead are being raised, and the gospel is being preached to the poor, as the prophets had foreseen. The powers of the kingdom of God were at work.

Jesus' ministry here on earth is described as "the days of the preaching of the kingdom of God" (Lk 16:16). When Jesus sent his disciples out on a mission, he commanded them to proclaim: "The kingdom of God has come near" (Lk 10:9). And when his critics asked him when the kingdom would finally come, he answered, "the kingdom of God is among you" (Lk 17:21). It was within their grasp, the door of the kingdom had been opened, all they needed to do was to go in. But, strangely, tax collectors and prostitutes were going into the kingdom before the members of the religious hierarchy (Mt. 21:32). Not only would they not enter God's kingdom, but they tried to prevent others from entering. "Woe to you scribes and Pharisees, hypocrites, for you lock people out of the kingdom of heaven; for you neither enter yourselves, nor allow those who enter to go in" (Mt 23:13).

In contrast to political kingdoms, which are established by force of arms, by a coup d'etat, by invading armies, the kingdom of God was to be established by Jesus, not only through his mighty deeds, his marvelous teachings, but above all, by his suffering and death. In the words of the poet: "The kingdoms of the earth go by, In purple and in gold; They rise, they flourish and they die, And all their tale is told. One kingdom only is divine, one banner triumphs still; Its king, a servant, and its sign, A gibbet on the hill" (G. F. Bradley). In the Latin version of a Psalm we read, "The Lord reigns from the tree." Indeed, he does!

The kingdom which Jesus inaugurated, however, was like a small mustard seed which, when planted, grows into a big shrub. It is subject to growth. In fact Jesus exhorts his disciples to pray, "Your kingdom come." His kingdom, which in the present is often opposed by evil powers, will in God's good time manifest itself in eternal glory. There is a future dimension to God's reign that will be realized when Christ returns to gather his elect from the earth. On that future day, the righteous, Christ's followers "will shine like the sun in the kingdom of their Father" (Mt 13:43).

I mention this future aspect of God's kingdom only because the presence of the kingdom is not yet the whole picture of God's reign. In the parables before us, however, the presence of the kingdom is in focus. And to discover this kingdom, both in the first as well as in the twenty-first century, is the most significant experience mortal human beings can have.

II. THE DISCOVERY OF THE KINGDOM

The two short parables before us illustrate how people discover the kingdom of God. A parable can, of course, never tell us everything about our salvation. Nothing is said here about hearing the gospel, about repentance from sin, about Christ's atoning death, about faith in him. He simply takes two pictures from everyday life to show how people discover God's kingdom.

A. The Treasure in the Ground

This parable may strike us as strange, but was perfectly natural to Jesus' hearers in Palestine. The ancient world did not have safety deposit boxes in banks, where one could stash away one's treasures, and those who hid their treasures in their private homes, could easily be robbed by thieves who, as Jesus sad, "dug through" and stole. Houses in those days were not built on concrete foundations or basements, and so it was not too hard to dig underneath the wall of a one-room house and to steal peoples' valuables. The safest place to keep one's treasures was to put them into an earthen pot and bury them in the ground. In one of Jesus' parables, we read of the unprofitable servant who hid his pound in the ground (Lk 19:20). In Palestine, where so many wars were fought, it was especially difficult to find a safe place to deposit one's valuables. The Jewish historian, Josephus, who lived about the time of Christ, tells us, that in the war that ended with the destruction of Jerusalem, many people hid their treasures in the ground, hoping to retrieve them after hostilities ceased. It happened during the chaos that followed the Russian Revolution (1917), when the Mennonite colonies in the Ukraine were often plundered, that people hid grain or flour or extra clothes in the ground.

Archaeologists have occasionally come upon treasure troves hidden in the ground or in caves. In the spring of 1947 two Bedouin lads were shepherding their sheep and goats at Qumran, by the cliffs of the Dead Sea. An animal went missing and so one of the boys threw a stone into a small cave in one of the rocky cliffs. When he heard what sounded like the breaking of crockery, he took fright. Later, however, the two of them crept into the cave, and there on its floor stuffed in jars, were rolls of crumbling leather manuscripts. They had made one of the biggest archaeological finds of modern times; they had discovered the Dead Sea Scrolls.

About two thousand years ago, Jesus, in his proclamation of the kingdom of God, told the story of a choice discovery of a treasure trove in the ground. He pictures a laborer ploughing a field, when suddenly the share of his plough lays bare a cache of precious coins. (Or perhaps his ox sank into the ground where the treasure was hidden.) We are not told who had hidden this treasure, whether it was the owner of the farm or some other unknown person. That kind of detail is not essential to the parable.

The laborer makes sure that no one has seen him unearthing a box of valuables (we assume it was coinage). He puts the box back and covers it up with ground, marking the spot. He is consumed by one desire: to obtain that treasure. And so he scrapes together or borrows the money, and he buys the entire field. Now the money is his. The parable doesn't go into the ethics of the man's behavior, although some rabbis evidently taught that the person who found money was allowed to keep it.

Here then we have a picture of someone who inadvertently stumbles upon treasure in the course of his daily activities. And so it happens in the lives of many people who are not overtly searching for God and his salvation. But suddenly something happens in the midst of their daily routine, that makes them aware of the kingdom of God. It is, of course, the Spirit of God that is at work in the lives of men and women. He seeks to draw them to the God who receives all those who come to him in faith. And, as they respond to the wooing of God's Spirit, their lives are turned upside down.

One well-known example of this kind of experience was that of C. S. Lewis, of literary fame. He was an agnostic, an Oxford don, who discovered the kingdom of God when he was not looking for it. In his autobiography he confesses, that he had settled for a materialistic universe in which God had no place and which had no meaning. But, as he puts it, "night after night, feeling whenever my mind lifted even for a second from my work, the steady unrelenting approach of him, whom I so earnestly desired not to meet. That which I greatly feared at last came upon me." In 1929 he capitulated, feeling himself to be the most reluctant convert in all of England. No prodigal, he confesses, ever dragged his feet so slowly into the Father's house as did he. He discovered the treasure in the field, and for the joy of this discovery, devoted his literary gifts to the defense of the Christian faith, and gave away a large portion of his income to the work of God's kingdom. No wonder he entitled his autobiography, ***Surprised by Joy.***

There are a great many Christian believers today who can witness to a similar experience. Something happened in their lives, or in the life of a loved one, that made them stop and face the ultimate questions of life. And by the grace of God they discovered the kingdom of God. However, there are also those who find the kingdom after a long search. And that aspect of discovering God's kingdom is illustrated in the second of the twin parables.

B. The Pearl of Great Value

Before us stands a merchant, a trader, whose consuming passion in life was to find precious pearls. Along with gold, pearls were considered to be of great value in Jesus' day. One needs only to read the book of Revelation to discover how important pearls were (Rev 18:16,17; 21:18-21). Before us then, is a man for whom the ordinary things of life have lost their attraction; he has one absorbing interest: pearls. He travels widely, perhaps to the Red Sea, Persia or India. He scours the markets of the Near East. He inquires of travelers and asks peddlers. His eyes are sharp; he knows how to distinguish between the genuine and the spurious pearls. Perhaps he already had a fine collection of pearls and found great delight in handling them and admiring them. If a friend or neighbor visited him, we can imagine that the conversation would quite regularly turn to "pearls."

And then one day something happened that made his collection seem so paltry and cheap. His eyes fell on a pearl such as he had never seen before, and before you knew it (the Greek verb represents the "dramatic perfect"), he liquidated all his possessions (not simply all his other pearls) and bought this pearl. And so it is, that people in whom God's Spirit is at work, who feel keenly that God-shaped vacuum in their lives, and who may have for years searched for the kingdom of God (either consciously or unknowingly), come upon the greatest treasure: the kingdom of God.

Dr. Emile Caillet, who came to America from France to teach French literature and then ended up as professor of theology at Princeton Theological Seminary, had the kind of experience the merchant in our parable had. As a young philosophy student in his native France he was convinced that philosophy had the answer to the deepest questions of human life. But during the First World War, as he lay in the trenches and saw his buddies die, he discovered that the little book into which he had written sayings of famous philosophers, was no help to his friends in the face of death. He then resolved that once the war was over, he would plunge deeper into philosophy, for he thought there had to be answers to the deep questions of human existence. Through a chance encounter with a Huguenot pastor, and through the reading of the New Testament (something he had never done before), he found the pearl of great value. And that made his former collection of "pearls" seem rather worthless. He began to delve into theology. In fact, he became an authority on the writings of the French scientist and theologian, Blaise Pascal. He had discovered the kingdom of God after a long search.

We should, however, not press the difference in the manner in which people discover the kingdom of God too much. What the two parables have in common is: that the discovery of the treasure of inestimable value led these men to give up everything they had in order to gain possession of their newly discovered treasure. The discovery of God's kingdom can be a costly experience, but our parables put the emphasis on the supreme value of the kingdom, and the joy that such a discovery elicits in peoples' lives.

III. THE SUPREME VALUE OF THE KINGDOM

The discovery of God's kingdom is another way of saying that we embrace God's reign over our hearts and lives. And this is not, as some might think, something burdensome. In fact in the parable of the treasure in the ground, it was the joy of the discovery that led this laborer to sell everything he had, so that he might be able to buy the entire field. The yoke of the kingdom, as Jesus put it, is easy and "my burden is light" (Mt 11:30).

When people submit to God's reign, the many discordant elements of their lives are brought into harmony. Often it happens, that latent gifts in the lives of individuals are released (or new gifts are given), with which they can serve in God's kingdom. It loosens our attachment to the material things of life. It changes our attitudes toward other people. It transforms our lives. It trans-values our former values. It gives our lives purpose and meaning and depth. It fills us with hope, since by faith we become members of a kingdom that ends in glory and lasts forever.

In Philippians 3, the apostle Paul gives us a short autobiography, in which he testifies to the supreme value of discovering God's kingdom. After listing a number of privileges and advantages which he had as a true Jew, he ends up with this confession: "Yet whatever gain I had, these I have come to regard as loss because of Christ. More than that, I regard everything as loss because of the surpassing value of knowing Christ Jesus my Lord. For his sake I have suffered the loss of all things, and I regard them as rubbish, in order that I may gain Christ" (Phil 3:7,8).

All over the world today, where the message of the kingdom of God is being heard, people are discovering that God's reign is of such value, that they are only sorry that they did not enter the kingdom sooner. In

19th century England lived Frederick Robertson, who became a great preacher of the gospel. But that had not been his original goal in life. He always wanted to be a soldier. Grandfather, father and all his brothers had been or were soldiers. He counted the years that must drag on before he could don the Queen's uniform and join the Dragoons. Strangely, as that long anticipated day drew closer, the Spirit of God was at work in his heart, and he discovered the treasure in the ground, the pearl of great value, and his former goals and ambitions faded into the background. His biographer writes, that when he finally became a minister of the gospel, his first service was a funeral service. It was his own funeral; he buried the soldier. All that had fired his youthful imagination had lost attraction in the light of the discovery of God's kingdom. He became a powerful witness to the grace of God in Brighton, England, and came to be known as "the preacher's preacher."

E. Stanley Jones, great Methodist missionary to India, and author of numerous books, came home to America on furlough. On one occasion he spent the night in a hotel in Alaska and there he saw himself in a mirror. As he looked at himself, he broke out in the following soliloquy: "Stanley, you are a very happy man, aren't you?" "Yes, I am." "And how did you get that way?" "I don't really know. It's all a surprise to me, a growing surprise. I walked across the field one day and I stubbed my toe against the edge of a treasure chest, jutting out of the earth." "It's a treasure, I cried out, and I ran off and sold everything I had, including myself, and bought that field. And I've been hugging myself ever since, that I had sense enough to do it." "Surprised by Joy!"

"Since then we have received an unshakable kingdom, let us have grace, by which to serve God in a well pleasing way" (Heb 12:28).

CHAPTER FOUR

THE GOOD SAMARITAN Luke 10:25~37

This woodcut is by an anonymous artist from Christoph Wiegel's **Biblia Ectypa: Bildnesse auss Heiliger Schrift, Alt und Neuen Testament** published in 1695.

THE GOOD SAMARITAN Luke 10:25-37

From the rich store of Jesus' teachings, Luke selects several stories that have Samaritans at their centre. He seems to manifest special interest in the downtrodden and the outcasts, to which the Samaritans belonged. Little love was lost between Jews and Samaritans in Jesus' day. If at all possible they avoided each other. In John's account of Jesus' encounter with the Samaritan woman at the well, he inserts this comment: "Jews do not share things in common with Samaritans" (Jn 4:9).

We who know this parable story don't find it all that shocking, but for the original Jewish audiences this story must have been very upsetting and disconcerting. The fact that a Samaritan turned out to be a true neighbor to the man who lay dying in the ditch, would have been hard for them to grasp. A Jewish expert in religious law asks Jesus to tell him who his neighbor is. Jesus doesn't answer that question; rather, he asks his Jewish audience to whom they thought this despised Samaritan was a neighbor. The answer to that question was, of course, unavoidable. And the parable ends with the exhortation: Go and do likewise!

In our effort to understand and to grasp the message of this parable, we want to begin by observing the occasion that led Jesus to tell this story. Secondly, we will focus on the compassionate Samaritan who becomes the model for Christian believers to imitate. And, thirdly, we want to see how Jesus applies this parable.

Attempts at classifying the parables of Jesus vary greatly. That they all revolve around the basic theme of Jesus' message, the kingdom of God, is generally accepted. But which aspect of the kingdom the individual parable stories illustrate, is not always so clear. Some parables speak of the coming of the kingdom in the person of Jesus, others of God's grace manifested in the coming of the Savior, still others point to the future consummation of the kingdom. However, there are a number of parables that describe how people who are members of God's kingdom are expected to live; they are ethical in their emphasis. The parable of the Good Samaritan would appear to fall into that category. Members of God's kingdom are to love God with all their heart and their neighbor as themselves. Let us then open our hearts to see what Jesus has to say to us about being good Samaritans!

I. THE OCCASION FOR THE PARABLE (10:25-29)

A. The Lawyer's Question (v. 25)

"Just then a lawyer stood up to test Jesus. 'Teacher,' he said, 'what must I do to inherit eternal life?'"

The word "lawyer" in everyday English has a different meaning from the word used in our parable. The Greek word **nomikos** means an expert in Jewish law, including both the written tradition (the Old Testament), as well as the oral tradition. If we were to look for a modern English equivalent, we might say "theologian," or "a student of the Scriptures," or "an expert in religion."

Jesus is on his way to Jerusalem, and an astute theologian confronts him with a question. He didn't ask because he didn't know the answer. He asked the question "to test" the Lord. He was eager to engage Jesus in argument, not because he was seeking for an answer to his question, but to put Jesus on the spot. Such people can be quite a bother, but Jesus is patient with him. The questioner was an authority on religious matters. By contrast, Jesus had not studied in the rabbinic schools in Jerusalem. This expert in Jewish theology may have wanted to examine Jesus to see whether his teachings were in agreement with Jewish theology. So we have a recognized theologian, examining an unofficial but extremely popular teacher, Jesus.

He addresses Jesus respectfully: "Teacher [i.e., rabbi} what must I do to inherit eternal life?" Eternal life is the life of the age to come; it is both qualitatively and quantitatively different from mere biological life, or life as we know it here on earth. It was a question not infrequently discussed among Jewish rabbis. The word "inherit" means simply to possess or to gain, but since eternal life in this context is thought of as lying in the future world, the word inherit is used.

B. Jesus' Counter-question (v. 16)

"He said to him, 'What is written in the law? what do you read there'?"

Had Jesus asked this question when he spoke to the common folk, he would have said, "Have you not heard?" Many people in those days could not read, and depended on the hearing of the word of God in the synagogue. But in this parable Jesus is addressing a trained scholar, and our Lord counters his question with: "What is written in the law? What do you read there?" He is pushing his interlocutor to answer his own question. And it should be noticed that Jesus is not interested in the oral tradition (sometimes called the tradition of the elders) that had been built up around the written word of God; he asks him to tell him what is written in the law, in the five books of Moses, the Pentateuch.

C. The Scholar's Reply (v. 27)

"He answered, 'You shall love the Lord your God with all your heart and with all your soul and with all your strength, and with all your mind, and your neighbor as yourself'."

The words which he quoted were part of Israel's confession of faith, called the **Shema**, which pious Jews recited daily. The first part of his quotation is found in Deuteronomy 6:5, and the last part in Leviticus 19:18. Love for God was obviously the highest good that anyone in Israel could attain to, and the Mosaic writer underscores this by piling up anthropological terms—heart, soul, strength, and mind. But where a person loves God with his or her whole being, this love will manifest itself in love for other people, as the Levitical text has it.

D. Jesus' Response (v. 28)

"And he said to him, 'You have given the right answer; do that and you will live'."

By now the roles have been reversed. The lawyer wanted to know if Jesus knew the right answer to his question. Jesus then compliments him on giving the correct answer. Indeed, at the heart of all true faith is love for God and this expresses itself in love for the neighbor. This is the teaching not only of the Old Testament but also of the New. How can someone say that he or she loves God, asks the apostle John, if he doesn't love his or her needy brother or sister (1 Jn 3:17). How can anyone love an unseen God when he or she fails to love the neighbor who can be seen?

E. The Lawyer's Retort (v. 29)

"But wanting to justify himself, he asked Jesus, 'And who is my neighbor'?."

The lawyer tried to gain the initiative; he wanted to save face. He looks rather foolish, having asked a question to which he had been forced to give the answer. In effect Jesus had told him, "You have no need to ask me the question about eternal life; as an expert in theology you know the answer. All you need to do is practice what you preach." However, he seemed to think, that he needed a clearer definition of who his neighbor was, before he could love his neighbor as himself, as God's word says.

The word "neighbor" was understood in more than one way in Judaism at the time of Jesus. (1) It was used, for example, of a fellow member of the Jewish community, the Jewish race. (ii) The Pharisees drew the circle even smaller; they tended to exclude even fellow Jews who were negligent when it came to the tradition of the elders and paid little attention to the niceties of Jewish customs. (iii) Completely outside the circle of neighbor love were the Gentiles. In the book of **Sirach** (12:1-7) we read, among other things, "Give to the godly person, but do not help the sinner...do not give to the ungodly. For the Most High also hates sinners."

In the Sermon on the Mount Jesus alludes to that restrictive view. "You have heard that it was said, 'Love your neighbor and hate your enemy'" (Mt 5:43). The last part of that statement, "hate you enemy," is not in the Scriptures; that had been added to indicate that some neighbors could be excluded. But Jesus will not allow that (Mt 5:44). There had been a marked influx of non-Jews in Palestine. Also, the Roman occupation forces were in the land, and travelers from Gentile lands visited in the holy land. Moreover, smack in the middle of the land lay Samaria, between Galilee in the north and Judea in the south. Here lived a people profoundly hated by Jews. And so the question, Who is my neighbor? was at times fiercely debated.

The theologian seemingly had no problem with the first of the two great commandments: loving God with all one's heart. Be he had a problem with the second: loving the neighbor as oneself. Evidently the lawyer had hoped Jesus would define the boundaries of what the word neighbor meant in the rather more narrow sense as he himself understood them. But he is in for a very unsettling surprise. Jesus responds by telling a story of a "good" Samaritan, which in Jewish thinking was an oxymoron.

II. THE COMPASSION OF THE SAMARITAN (vv. 30-37)

A. Jews and Samaritans Generally

Jesus could not have chosen a more unlikely person to illustrate how comprehensive the word "neighbor" actually was in God's sight. Jews avoided all contact with Samaritans. The enemies of Jesus on one occasion, when they couldn't think of anything worse to call Jesus, said he was a Samaritan (Jn 8:48). Jews traveling between Judea and Galilee regularly avoided going through Samaria. They preferred to go along the eastern border of Samaritan territory.

Although they had much in common with the Jews, including the Pentateuch, Jews regarded Samaritans as semi-foreigners. They thought of them as a mixed race, for when the northern kingdom went into captivity in the 8th century, the Assyrians brought in Eastern peoples which presumably mixed with the left-over Jewish population. When the Jewish exiles returned from their Babylonian captivity in the 4th century B.C., the Samaritans offered to help them in the rebuilding of the temple in Jerusalem. However, they were rebuffed by the Jews and that created great animosity.

The Samaritans then went ahead and built their own temple on Mt. Gerizim, and that was a thorn in the eyes of the Jews. This temple was destroyed in 128 B.C., when the Jews asserted their independence during the Maccabean wars, under the leadership of John Hyrcanus.. Eventually the animosity between Jews and Samaritans became so intense that a petition, asking God to prohibit Samaritans from inheriting eternal life, was made part of synagogue prayers. The coming of the Roman governors in A.D. 6, who had their seat in Caesarea on the coast, brought some relief to the Samaritans. At least they were now free from the rule of the Herodians. But clashes between Jews and Samaritans continued. On one occasion some Samaritans snuck into the Jerusalem temple before Passover and scattered human bones in the sanctuary, making the temple unclean and unfit for the festival.

Given this background, we can appreciate the controversial nature of Jesus' introduction of a Samaritan into this parable. Those who listened in on the dialogue between Jesus and the lawyer may well have appreciated the negative portrait of the priest and the Levite in the parable, for there was a lot of anti-clericalism among the common folk. Perhaps they expected that an ordinary Jewish lay person would come to the aid of the poor man who had fallen among the thieves, and put the "clergy" to shame. But it was a Samaritan who came to the rescue of the victim. By the time Jesus had finished the story, both the lawyer and the wider audience must have squirmed. Let us then turn to the story!

B. Tragedy On the Way to Jericho (v. 30)

"A man was going down from Jerusalem to Jericho, and fell into the hands of robbers, who stripped him, beat him, and went away, leaving him half dead."

The road from Jerusalem to Jericho is only 27 kms long, and it drops about 1,200 meters. It was a road marked by limestone cliffs and gullies, and because it was a dangerous road, it was known as the "path of blood." In the 12th century the Crusader Order of Templars was founded to protect pilgrims traveling this way. And when the Ottoman Turks ruled Palestine, in the 19th century, pilgrims were often given an escort of Turkish soldiers for the journey between Jerusalem and Jericho.

The road was heavily traveled by pilgrims and caravans; and bandits frequently hid behind the limestone rocks and attacked travelers. In our story the man who was attacked by robbers is not identified. Whether he was rich or poor, whether he was a Jew or non-Jew, is not stated, and that is quite immaterial to the thrust of the parable. All that is said is, that he went down from Jerusalem to Jericho.

One should read no significance into the "going down," for everyone who went to Jericho went down, and to Jerusalem one had to go up.

At one point between Jerusalem and Jericho a band of brigands, bandits, robbers, attacked a pedestrian who was on his way to Jericho. Perhaps he resisted, and so they tore off his clothes and beat him half to death. Whether he was carrying any money or not is not stated, but obviously that's what the robbers were after. They left him lying beside the road, in the ditch, as we would say, half dead. How long he lay there in his misery is not said. Finally other travelers came along.

C. The Response of the Religious Leaders (vv. 31,32)

"Now by chance a priest was going down that road; and when he saw him he passed by on the other side."

Since he was "going down," we assume he was also on his way to Jericho. Many priests lived in Jericho—a city with a warm winter climate. Jericho lies in the fertile Jordan Valley and was famous for its date-palm plantations. Since there were so many priests, they took their turn at serving in the temple for only a few weeks of the year. The rest of the year they lived in Jericho. Very likely this particular priest was returning home after completing his religious duties in the temple.

He took one look at the half-dead man and then passed on. If he was riding a donkey, he didn't bother to get off. Why?

We're not told. Some think he was afraid that the robbers were still hiding close by and that he might be their next victim, and so he wanted to get away as quickly as possible. But there was possibly another reason: he may have felt that touching a half-dead man would make him ritually unclean. It may in fact have appeared to him, that the man was dead. According to Leviticus 19, after touching a corpse, a priest had to be purified, and that took an entire week. That might have been an excuse if he had been on his way to the temple in Jerusalem for a week of services, but this man was going to Jericho. But, whether he was afraid of being robbed or whether he feared ritual contamination, the priest is portrayed as a callous individual, a man who showed no concern for the neighbor, and Jesus does not excuse him.

Some time later another representative of the religious establishment comes along: a Levite. "So likewise a Levite, when he came to the place and saw him, passed by on the other side" (v. 32). Had he seen what the priest had done and decided to follow his example? We don't know how far behind the priest he was. Levites had an inferior position to that of priests. They were responsible for some aspects of the temple liturgy, such as the music. Also, the policing of the temple was in their hands. Both priests and Levites were quite literally a class apart in Jewish society, and they were expected to observe high ethical standards. Both of them, however, are portrayed in our parable as moral failures. And now comes the shocking turn in the story.

D. The Compassion of the Samaritan (vv. 33-35)

"But a Samaritan while traveling came near him; he was moved with pity. He went to him and bandaged his wounds, having poured oil and wine in them. Then he put him on his own animal, brought him to an inn, and took care of him."

Jesus' audience no doubt would have been pleased if a Jewish lay person had shown mercy to the victim, but Jesus introduces a man who wasn't even a member of the Jewish community. Samaritans were classified with Edomites and Philistines. In Sirach 50:25,26 we read: "With two nations my soul [i.e., God's soul] is vexed and the third is not a nation. Those who live on Mt Seir [i.e., the Edomites] and the Philistines, and the foolish people that dwells in Shechem [i.e., the Samaritans)."

There was nothing strange about a Samaritan traveling along this road, just as Jews did upon occasion travel through Samaria, even though that was always a bit dangerous. This man was not on his way home to Samaria, as verse 35 clearly indicates. But when he saw this half-dead man, lying beside the road, he had compassion on him; he was moved to the depths of his inner being. (The Greek verb **splagchnizomai** is very vivid. It suggests that his whole inner being, his **splagchna** [viscera] were stirred up.)

His pity expressed itself, first, in that he bandaged his wounds, pouring oil and wine in them. We assume the Samaritan was riding a donkey and had some equipment for the journey with him. Oil and wine was a kind of first-aid kit; the oil served as ointment, and the wine as disinfectant, as an antiseptic. Showing compassion and binding up wounds is how God is portrayed in the Old Testament. He heals the broken hearted and binds up their wounds (Ps 147:3). "He has struck us down; he will bind us up" (Hos 6:1). The priest and Levite must have known that that was what God did, and that they should imitate the God of Israel, to whom they confessed loyalty.

But that was not all that the Samaritan did. He lifted him up and put him on "his own animal." He too must have known that robbers could pounce on him at any moment. A man on a donkey would have been an attractive object for highway robbery. Samaritans who observed the laws of the Pentateuch, also knew that contact with the dead caused ritual impurity. Moreover, by bringing this half-dead man to Jericho, he could have been suspected of being an accomplice in the crime.

But the Samaritan let none of these considerations deter him from exercising compassion. Whether he walked beside the donkey, steadying the half-dead victim, is not stated, but he brought him to an inn in Jericho and cared for him. We assume he nursed him for the rest of the day.

"The next day he took out two ***denarii***, gave them to the innkeeper, and said, 'Take care of him and when I come back, I will repay you whatever more you spend' (v.35)". If the poor man had any money when he left Jerusalem, the robbers would certainly have relieved him of that; he was obviously penniless. So the Samaritan paid for him. A ***denarius*** was a day's wage. He gave the innkeeper two ***denarii***. Just how many days' expenses that would have covered is not altogether certain, but he promised to make up the rest upon his return.

The next day he had to leave; no doubt he was on business. And that's where the curtain falls, as far as the story goes. No more needed to be said about this compassionate Samaritan.

III. THE APPLICATION (vv. 3 6,37)

In many of the parables of Jesus, the hearers had to make the application of the truth or truths themselves. In this parable, however, Jesus rounds the story off by making the application. An expert in Jewish law had asked a question. Jesus answered his question with an unsettling story. And he asked his interlocutor the question: "Which of these three do you think was a neighbor to the man who fell into the hands of the robbers?" This theologian had actually asked: "Who is my neighbor?" But Jesus asks: "To whom was this Samaritan a neighbor?" There was no way this expert in Jewish religion could weasel out; the bystanders were listening in; he couldn't lose face. And so he replied: "the one who showed mercy." Notice that he couldn't get himself to say, "the Samaritan." That would have been just too odious. Jesus then tells him: "Go and do likewise!"

It was a courageous act on the part of Jesus to tell a story about a good Samaritan in the presence of Jewish hearers who hated and despised the Samaritans. A missionary who spent 20 years in the Near East, writes, that he had not had the courage in all those years to tell Palestinians a story about a noble Israeli; nor had he ever told Armenians a story about a noble Turk (the Turks massacred thousands of Armenians during the First World War). He said that it would have been too dangerous. But Jesus proclaims God's message without fear, and drives home important truths, uncomfortable though they may be.

There is much in this parable that is left unsaid. Who the robbers were is not stated. They don't need to be identified. The same can be said of the unfortunate victim. Was he Jew or Gentile? Was he Pharisee, Sadducee, Essene or Zealot? Perhaps he was one of the so-called "people of the land." All that is of no significance for the parable to stab our consciences. And the same holds true for the priest and the Levite. Their calling is mentioned, but nothing is said about the individuals themselves. We don't know their names or what they did when they were on or off duty at the temple. We know nothing about their families, either. All we can safely assume is, that they lived in Jericho and that they failed miserably in the face of human need that cried for help.

Also, we know nothing about the innkeeper. Was he generous or did he overcharge the Samaritan? Apparently it made no difference to him that a Samaritan delivered a half-dead man, whom he had picked up at the roadside, to his inn. All these people are simply part of the staging, the scenery, the backdrop of the story. The parable focuses entirely on one individual: the Samaritan. He is the chief actor on this stage; he is the main character. He knows what to do and does it. Race, religion, and class distinctions do not determine whether he will come to the aid of a suffering human being. He stopped his donkey and stooped to tend the suffering victim. He didn't ask whether he was Jew, Roman, Greek or Syrian. A naked, wounded, half-dead man was in need, and that was all that mattered.

The Samaritan paid for the victim's keep at the inn. And he didn't expect this poor fellow to pay him back some day, after he recovered. We don't even know whether the wounded man expressed his gratitude to the Samaritan for saving his life.

This Samaritan, so despised by the Jews, went to great lengths to save a needy person; he risked his own safety; he sacrificed his own comfort; he accepted the interruption in his travel plans; he spent hours in loving service and watchful care. All this effort cost him time, energy and money. But nothing deterred him.

The Jewish theologian wanted to know where to draw the line when it came to loving the neighbor. Jesus shows us that there is no limit to love and kindness. The neighbor in this story was not an attractive person. He was covered with blood, helpless and half-dead. But no one can claim to love God and at the same time pass by callously when a fellow human being is in need. As we tune our hearts to absorb the message of this parable story, let us heed the words of the apostle James about being doers of the word and not hearers only (Jam 1:22).

CHAPTER FIVE

THE UNJUST STEWARD Luke 16:1-13

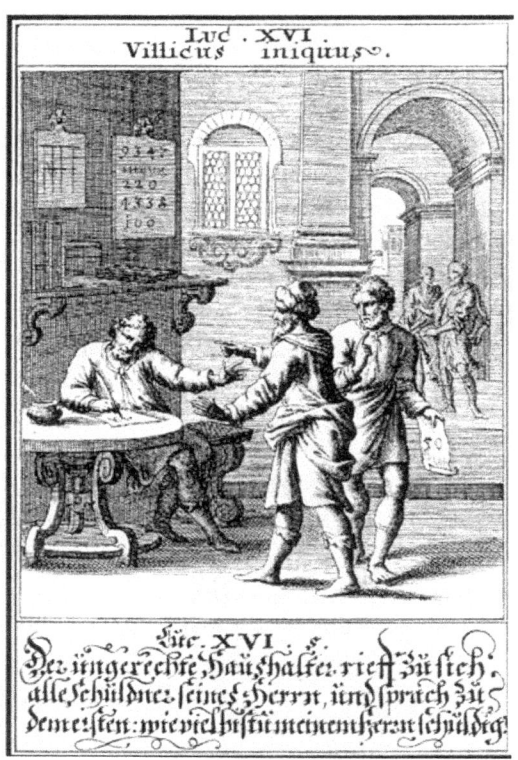

This woodcut is by an anonymous artist from Christoph Wiegel's **Biblia Ectypa: Bildnesse auss Heiliger Schrift, Alt und Neuen Testament** published in 1695.

THE UNJUST STEWARD Luke 16:1-13

It goes without saying that this parable is one of the most perplexing of all the parables of Jesus. It speaks of a bad man's good example. The story itself is simple enough. A landowner has entrusted the management of his farms into the hands of a steward, a manager. The manager was charged with squandering his master's property. He is called upon to produce the records of income and expenditures. This puts him in an awkward position. He knows this will cost him his job, and so he decides to pull off one more enormous rip-off. The original readers of this parable no doubt expected Jesus to denounce this scoundrel, to rebuke him and condemn him for his dishonesty. Instead, he drives home a lesson for his disciples on the use of money.

There are always those who say that this is not a parable, but that it is an account of something that actually happened. It most certainly is true to life. It's the kind of thing that happened again and again in Jesus' day. But when a story is told to drive home an important spiritual or moral truth, it is called a parable. We must remind ourselves, that the Hebrew word for parable (***mashal***) covers the whole field of illustrations. Every published book in the parables of Jesus includes also the parable of the unjust steward.

What has always puzzled interpreters is, that Jesus should take a man who turns out to be an embezzler, to teach his followers an important lesson about material things. In the early centuries of the Christian church, when allegory was popular, attempts were made to identify all the details of the story, and in that way some of the embarrassing aspects of the parable were overcome. Theophulus of Antioch, in the last 2nd century, suggested that Paul was the unjust steward who had squandered his Lord's goods when, in his unbelief, he had persecuted the church. In the end, however, the Lord commended him for replacing the harshness of the Jewish law, which led him to harass Christians, with the kindness of the gospel, after he became a believer. But there were other attempts to identify the unjust steward. Some thought he was Judas, or even Satan.

But by arbitrarily identifying the details of the story, the pointed teachings of the parable are lost. Jesus wants his disciples to be good stewards, and that's the burden of the story. Martin Luther wrote: "Let us not fall into the error of imagining that everything in the story is significant. If we did, we would be encouraging people to go about cheating their masters as the steward did. No, the point to fasten on, is the cleverness of the steward who saw his own advantage and so well and wisely achieved it." His contemporary, John Calvin, wrote: "How stupid it is to want to interpret every detail. Christ simply meant that the children of this world are more diligent in their concern for their own fleeting interest, than the sons of light for their eternal well-being." In his commentary on Luke he wrote: "We must treat our neighbors humanely and kindly, so that when we come before God's judgment seat, we may receive the fruit of our liberality." Such were the views of the two leading 16th century reformers.

Let us then be clear on one thing: this parable was not told to teach people how to juggle accounts for their own advantage. Today we often hear of companies that indulge in what is sometimes called "creative accounting." This parable is not an encouragement to "cook the books," as we say. Jesus does not condone embezzlement. The manager in our story is not held up as a model in business ethics; in fact, it is clearly indicated that he acted unethically. But Jesus lets some divine light shine through the clever machinations of this unjust manager, that can serve as a guide for members of the kingdom of God, the Christian believers.

There is a world of difference between applauding

an unjust manager for his shrewdness, his farsightedness, and applauding his dishonesty. The story itself is just part of the staging, the backcloth, through which Jesus gives his followers instructions on how to view earthly possessions, wealth, and other gifts that God graciously bestows upon his people.

Although verse 1 states that Jesus was talking to his disciples when he told this story, we should notice that verse 14 adds something interesting: "When the Pharisees heard this, they scoffed, for they were lovers of money." There was, then, a wider audience as well. Let us now get the story before us!

I. THE STORY (vv. 1-8a)

A. The Landlord and His Manager (vv. 1,2)

"Then Jesus said to the disciples, There was a rich man who had a manager, and charges were brought to him that this man was squandering his property. So he summoned him and said to him, 'What is this I hear about you? Give me an accounting of your management, because you can not be manager any longer'."

In the background of this parable stands an oriental landlord. He is the owner of farms. In Galilee agriculture was big business in Jesus' day. Galilean society was largely agrarian and wealthy land owners were putting small farmers out of business by buying more and more land. The land owner in our story was well to do: "there was a rich man." There is another parable in this 16th chapter of Luke which begins in exactly the same way: "there was a rich man" (v. 19). No Gospel writer has so much to say about money as does Luke. Also, Luke shows great interest in the poor. Although the Gospel writers all draw upon material that goes back to Jesus, they are selective in what they choose from the vast reservoir of Jesus' teachings. And so we can say, that each writer puts his own stamp on these teachings, under the guidance of the holy Spirit.

We are not given any information about this rich man. We are not told whether he was a good man or bad man. We don't even know whether he gained his wealth by hard work and careful planning or by inheritance. Nor is it stated that he customarily drove hard bargains with his tenants. All that is of no significance as far as the basic teaching of the parable goes. This rich man may have lived at some distance from his estates, his lands. He may have lived in a village or a city, or even in a villa by the seashore. He had entrusted the supervision of his farms to a steward. The Greek word for steward is **oikonomos**, from which we have derived our word "economy." In Jesus' day an **oikonomos** could be a secretary, a business manager, a trustee, an agent, or a treasurer. In current English he might even be called a broker or attorney.

In our parable he is the middle man, the broker, the go-between of a wealthy landowner and his clients who farmed his lands. This manager would be responsible for leasing the farms to tenants, for collecting the produce, for keeping records of income and disbursements. He might have been a salaried manager, who received a fixed sum annually, or he might have received a percentage of the income from crops. Perhaps he even received kickbacks from grateful renters. In any case, he is accused of squandering his master's property, and he doesn't protest the accusation. His silence seems to confirm, that he was guilty.

The owner of these farms, to begin with, must have felt, that his property was in good hands and that he was sure of a good income. He could bask in the sunshine on a Mediterranean beach without any worries. His lands were in good hands. He didn't have to bother his head about the tenants or about the everyday operation of his farms.

But then he hears rumors that something is wrong.

Had the crops failed or had the tenants complained about the high rent his manager was charging them? In any case, they had fallen behind in their payments and were now deeply in debt. The parable lays no blame at the feet of the tenants; it is the manager who is described as "unjust." He is charged, accused of mismanagement. The word "charged" does not necessarily mean that he was slandered, or accused falsely. He is charged with being a swindler, an embezzler.

As far as we know, the owner did not investigate the charges, to see if they were in fact true. He simply asks the manager to turn over the books, the records, the accounts. According to the laws of that day, he could have been thrown into prison. Imprison-ment for reneging on debt repayment was a common practice. In our story, the owner simply fires the manager. And the manager makes no attempt to clear his name or to defend himself. He knew that the charges were only too true. His master is not about to reverse his decision. In the eyes of the villagers the manager will be put to shame.

He is now in a very miserable situation. In a few days he will be without a job; he'll be out on the street, as it were. He would very likely not be able to pick up a comparable job. There weren't that many managerial jobs available, and no one would want to employ a man who had proved to be a crook anyway.

As manager he had become accustomed to a soft life, and so as he considers his options, he knows that he is not strong enough to handle pick and shovel; his body wouldn't take that. So how will he keep body and soul together? Very likely he had a family to feed. How would he put bread on the table for himself and his loved ones? Should he go begging? No, that was considered too shameful in oriental society. For a former manager to go begging was too great a disgrace. In the Jewish book of **Ecclesiasticus** (40:28), known also as "The Wisdom of Jesus Ben Sirach," we read: "It is better to die than to beg." Besides the shame and the loss of his livelihood there was probably also a lot of anger in his heart at his boss. And so we hear the manager talking to himself. Soliloquy is not uncommon in parables. We heard the prodigal son in Luke 15 talking to himself, before he decided to return to his father.

B. The Manager's Scheme (vv. 3.-7)

"Then the manager said to himself, 'What will I do, now that my master is taking the position away from me? I am not strong enough to dig, and I am ashamed to beg. I have decided what to do, so that when I am dismissed as manager, people may welcome me into their homes.' So, summoning his master's debtors one by one, he asked the first, 'How much to you owe my master?' He answered, 'A hundred jugs of olive oil.' He said to him, 'Take your bill, sit down quickly, and make it fifty.' Then he asked another, 'And how much do you owe?' He replied, 'A hundred containers of wheat.' He said to him, 'Take your bill and make it eighty'."

I suppose he could have squeezed as much out of his tenants as possible, but he decides on a different plan. A brilliant idea stirs in his mind. "I know what I will do." No doubt he said that with a gleam in his eye. "I have a great idea, I will reduce the debts of my tenants." Some scholars have suggested that he was not really dishonest in planning this approach, but that he was simply giving up his own commission or canceling the interest on the debts the tenants owed. But Jesus clearly calls him unrighteous, unjust.

The tenants of course would not have known that the manager was being relieved of his post and dealt with him in good faith. His plan had several advantages: (a) The debtors would be forever grateful to him for such kindness; they would look on him as a friend and benefactor from now on. And when he lost his job, they would certainly be willing to help him out. (b) Another possible advantage was, that by lowering the debts of his tenants, they may have been encouraged to pay up. All that would, of course, have gone into his own pockets, and he would have had some resources after he left his post.

So he decides to call them in, one by one. How many he called we do not know, only two examples are given. There may well have been more. One of them owed him 100 *baths* of olive oil. One *bath* was about 8 gallons. In other words, 800 gallons of olive oil. This would be the produce, so it is estimated, of about 150 olive trees. When it comes to weights and measures in the Bible, we always have to allow for a margin of inaccuracy, as far as modem equivalents are concerned. In terms of money, this would be about 1000 *denarii*, thinks the German scholar J. Jeremias in his book on parables. A *denarius* was a day's wage in those days. So that was a huge debt. He offers to cut it in half.

The other man owed him 100 *kor* of grain. One *kor* is ten bushels. So, a 1000 bushels of wheat! In Palestine in the first century that might be the produce of 100 acres, since crop yields in those days were relatively low. In terms of money, some estimate, that a 1000 bushels of wheat would be worth 2,500 *denarii*. This man's debt is reduced from 100 *kor* of wheat to 80. That amounts to about the same amount of reduction for each debtor in monetary terms. (*Bath* and *kor* are Hebrew words, the former for a liquid, the latter for a dry measure.)

You can imagine how overwhelmed these tenants must have been with the generosity of the manager and with what joy these tenants left his office. Had he tried to squeeze them for immediate repayment, they would have been his enemies, but now they became his friends. And friendship in the Near East is generally valued more highly than in the western world. Friends were under obligation to help each other in need.

The manager was a crook, a swindler; he was unjust. It may even be that the tenants were mired in debt because he had charged exorbitant rents. There is a rabbinic saying that goes like this: "When a man possesses a farm, he gives it to a tenant for half, or third, or quarter [of the crop]. But God does not act that way. He sends the wind, the rain, permits roses to grow and plants, and fruits to ripen, and demands no more than a tenth." This saying simply illustrates the high rents that landlords occasionally levied of their tenants.

C. The Master's Commendation (v. 8a)

"And his master commended the dishonest manager because he had acted shrewdly."

We have a problem with the word "master" in this verse (Greek has *kurios*, i.e. lord), because the word could refer either to the landowner or to Jesus who is telling the parable. (a) If the word refers to the landlord, then he seems to be praising his manager, not for his mismanagement, but for his shrewdness, not for his ethics, but for the smart way in which he assured himself a future. (b) If, on the other hand, the word "lord" refers to Jesus' valuation of the manager, we would have to say, that Jesus did not praise him for his unrighteousness, but for the man's cleverness in providing for his future. Not his dishonesty, but his far-sightedness is praised. In the ancient Syriac Version (the first translation of the Greek NT), the text reads, "Our Lord" praised the unjust steward. That makes it clear that these translators thought this commendation was spoken by Jesus. However, the Greek leaves that open, and it is hard to decide between these two views.

The argument that our Lord could not have praised such a corrupt manager, does not hold, for he is not commending him for his unrighteousness only for his foresight. He calls him an "unjust steward." The manager is clearly a man of this world and not a disciple of Jesus. On the other hand, it is something that his landlord could also have said, angry though he must have been at being betrayed by a man he had trusted. He might have said, "What a clever fox that manager of mine is; that guy is smart."

But, whether it is the landlord or Jesus speaking in the first half of verse 8, when we come to the second half, it is clearly our Lord who is speaking. (It should be remembered that there were no verse divisions in the original manuscripts.)

II. THE OBSERVATION (v. 8b)

"For the children of this age are more shrewd in dealing with their own generation than the children of light."

Literally the text speaks of "the sons of this age" and "the sons of light." Since to be a son of something is a Semitism and is often used in an inclusive sense, modem English versions usually speak of "children of this age." To be a son of something means to be characterized by whatever one is a son of. For example, people might be called sons of wrath, sons of disobedience, sons of Belial, and the like. "Sons of this age" are worldlings. We might call them unbelievers. However, Jesus is not saying that all unbelievers cheat. No, many of them are honest and upright. That is not under discussion here.

Sons of this age are thought of as being in darkness. By contrast, believers are "sons of light." Paul also speaks of the "sons of light" or "sons of the day" (1 Thess 5:5). Jesus seems to be suggesting that this "son of this age," this worldling, this unrighteous manager, was wiser than some of the children of light. Jesus did not excuse his dishonesty; dirty hands are called dirty; sin is sin; the wisdom of this age is never equated with godliness. And so we can be sure, this parable in no way runs counter to what Jesus taught about justice, honesty and integrity.

But what did he mean when he said the children of the present age are shrewder than the children of light? Here we have a dishonest man who looks ahead and knows that soon he will be without any financial resources. He will need friends who will take him and his family into their houses. And so he makes friends with the mammon of unrighteousness and in that way he secures his future.

But we ask, Do not Christ's followers also plan for their future here on earth? Of course they do. And Jesus is not criticizing Christians for planning for old age. The elderly don't want to be a burden to others, and they don't want to go on welfare either. In what sense then are they less astute than the children of this age? Let us be clear on one thing: Jesus is not praising worldliness. But he recognizes that wordlings are often more astute in dealing with their own kind, as the text has it. The manager was dealing with his own kind, in the sense that he was negotiating a monetary deal that would secure him and his family an immediate future here on earth. By implication, Jesus seems to express the wish, that the children of light might be as bent on eternal treasures, as the children of this age are, when it comes to their earthly welfare. This manager grabbed the opportunity to secure for himself a future here on earth. Should not the children of light, whose lives are oriented to the age to come, be as eager to seize the opportunities to gain eternal values? These eternal values are called "friends" in verse 9, and that may suggest that Jesus has the needy who need help in mind.

III. THE EXHORTATION (v. 9)

"The word "mammon" is an Aramaic word for "wealth." By itself it is neutral in its meaning. However, when it is described as the "mammon of unrighteousness," then it has taken on a rather pejorative meaning. There is a lot of unrighteousness connected with the gaining of mammon, the saving of mammon, and the using of mammon. But does this mean that Christians should have nothing to do with mammon? No, we need it to live our daily lives here on earth. Our text doesn't say, Keep your hands off it! It says the exact opposite. Take it in hand and do something with it! Exchange it for eternal values!

Paul writes to the Ephesians, "Let the thief no longer steal; but rather let him labor, doing honest work with his hands, so that he may be able to give to those in need" (4:28). That's how believers can make friends with the mammon to which so much unrighteousness is attached. Also, the apostle instructs the well-to-do in the church not to put their trust in their wealth, which is uncertain, but rather in God, who furnishes us richly with everything to enjoy. But then he adds: "To do good, to be rich in good deeds, liberal and generous, thus laying up for themselves a good foundation for the future, so that they may take hold of the life which is life indeed" (1 Tim 6:17-19). No doubt that's what Jesus meant when he spoke of laying up treasure in heaven

The day will come, says Jesus in our parable, when mammon will fail. In some older English versions we have a different reading: "When they fail." But the better manuscripts have "when it [i.e., **mammon**] fails." The Greek verb ***ekleipo*** (to fail), has given us our word "eclipse." Some day, if not during our life-time, then certainly when we die, all our possessions will be eclipsed. The NRSV has "when it is gone." We brought nothing into this world and we will take nothing out when we die. There are no pockets in a shroud, as the saying goes. However, if we have invested in the kingdom of God, which never passes away, we will be rewarded.

When mammon is gone, they will receive us into the eternal tents. Commentators are not agreed on who the "they" are. Some think the angels will welcome us. No doubt they will, but is that what Jesus meant? Others suggest the friends we have made, by being good steward of our mammon, will welcome us. Still others suggest that the "they" is a reference to God. Jesus often used substitutes or circumlocutions for God. By being good stewards of the gifts with which God has entrusted us, God will give us a joyous welcome in the world to come.

To be received in "the eternal tents," is a way of speaking of heaven, in contrast to the transitory homes here on earth. The concept of living in tents goes back to the early days of Israel's history, when the people lived in tents during their long journey through the wilderness. And to commemorate that period in the life of the old people of God, the festival of Booths, of tents, of tabernacles, was celebrated in the autumn of each year. During this week-long festival the people lived in makeshift shelters, booths. The tent represented a temporary dwelling place. By adding the adjective "eternal" to the word tent, it was used to designate the heavenly dwelling place of the righteous. John, in the Revelation, promises his readers that in the world to come God will spread his tent over them (7:15). And when John saw the new Jerusalem coming out of heaven down upon the new earth, he broke out in the words, "Behold, the tabernacle [the tent] of God among men" (21:3).

Imagine coming home to glory and meeting friends from all over the world, people whom we have never met here in life but, because of our faithful stewardship, they heard the gospel, received food and clothing and medical help. And when we speak of stewardship we should not think only of money, but also of other gifts that we can invest in God's kingdom, such as our time, our energy, our gifts, our skills, our education, with which we can make friends.

The story is told, that when David Livingstone's body was brought home to London for burial, one of his former classmates stood among the crowds that thronged the streets to watch the funeral cortege move by. And, as he saw the thousands who had come to witness the passing of a man who had spent his life for Africa, he was overheard to say: "I guess I put the emphasis on the wrong world."

And with that we come to a kind of addendum, attached to this parable, in which Jesus has some more important things to say about stewardship. I will call that the application and the warning.

IV. THE APPLICATION AND WARNING (vv. 10-13)

A. The Application (vv. 10-12)

"Whoever is faithful in a very little is faithful also in much; and whoever is dishonest in a very little is dishonest also in much. If then you have not been faithful with the unrighteous mammon, who will entrust to you true riches? And if you have not been faithful with what belongs to another, who will give you what is your own."

It is generally true that people who are conscientious and faithful in little things, will also be trustworthy when it comes to greater things. Life is made up largely of smaller things, and the real test of character is seen in the less significant, every-day things of life. However, in our context the reference is specifically to material possessions. In the light of eternity money is a triviality, and should not be over-valued. Nevertheless, our use of money is a measure of our faithfulness as followers of Jesus. Moreover, the person who uses his or her possessions and gifts the wrong way, is unfit to handle the more important things, the riches of God's kingdom, genuine wealth, spiritual wealth.

To be unfaithful with the mammon of unrighteousness would mean to hoard one's wealth, to be greedy, not knowing when enough is enough, or to spend it foolishly on a lavish lifestyle. Such people will not be entrusted with true riches. Some take the true riches to refer to spiritual wealth, the riches of faith, or even the gospel itself. We have had many embarrassing examples in our generation of ministers of the gospel who lost the trust of their people, because they were found to be unfaithful in money matters. There are other scholars who go so far as to say, that when greed and selfishness determines a person's everyday life, such a person might even forfeit his or her place in the heavenly kingdom. Here is what Paul writes to the Ephesians: "Be sure of this, that no fornicator, or impure person, or one who is greedy (that is, an idolator), has any inheritance in the kingdom of Christ and God" (Eph *5:5)*. Also, in 1 Corinthians 6:10 he writes, that the greedy will not inherit the kingdom of God.

What is said in verse 11 is given in another form in verse 12: "And if you have not been faithful with what belongs to another, who will give you what is your own?" Here Jesus explains that material possessions don't really belong to us. They belong to God. They have been given to us in trust. We are to be stewards of God's gifts. But if we are not trustworthy with what doesn't belong to us (i.e., material things), then how do we expect to receive what is our own (i.e., the treasures of the kingdom of God, both present and future)?

B. The Warning (v. 13)

"No slave can serve two masters, for he will either hate the one and love the other, or be devoted to the one and despise the other. You cannot serve God and mammon."

This saying does not mean that a person today could not work faithfully at two different jobs, or have two different bosses. But a slave is expected to give exclusive loyalty to the master who owns him or her. The expressions "love" and "hate," found in this verse, are often used as figures of speech in Semitic languages, to express strong rejection or strong preference. We cannot serve God and be enslaved to mammon at the same time. (Mammon is here personified.) To serve mammon is idol worship. It is not that the mammon itself is evil, but, as Paul puts it, "the love of money is a root of all kinds of evil" (1 Tim 6:10).

Dr. Raymond Edman was for many years president of Wheaton College. He was a great inspiration to me when I was a student there. Shortly before his death he wrote an article in which he recalled two occasions when he had been at death's door. Once when he came home deathly sick from the mission field in Latin American, the other when he had a heart attack while traveling in the Near East. In recalling these two events, he says, that he had had no fear of death in those critical moments. However, in both instances his whole life had passed by in review, and it seemed to him that three things stood out: salvation, service and stewardship. In those dark moments he had had no question about his salvation. He had the deep assurance that his sins were forgiven and that he was accepted by God. In the matter of service, well, that was different. There was still much to be done, so much that was unfinished, so much, perhaps, that would not stand the test in the presence of God. However, when it came to stewardship (and this surprised me), his heart was glad. Here's what he wrote: "Over the years I have loved the Lord's work and have been glad to share with his people in his glad service. Prayer and planning went into stewardship, and there was much gladness in giving."

May we also be found to have been good stewards of the gifts which God has entrusted to us!

CHAPTER SIX

THE WEEDS AMONG THE WHEAT
Matthew 13:24-30; 36-43

This woodcut is by an anonymous artist from Christoph Wiegel's **Biblia Ectypa: Bildnesse auss Heiliger Schrift, Alt und Neuen Testament** published in 1695.

THE WEEDS AMONG THE WHEAT Matthew 13:24-30; 36-43

This agricultural parable is unique to Matthew. And, like the parable of the soils, which is found in all three Synoptic Gospels, this parable was spoken by Jesus first to crowds of people, and then, later, after they had gone into a house, he explained its meaning in greater detail for his disciples (Mt. 13:36). After listening to Jesus speak repeatedly about the inbreaking of the kingdom of God, people may have wondered whether there was any concrete evidence that the kingdom was in fact being established. After all, evil was still rampant, the Romans were still in the land, and there were no indications that their rule would come to an end soon. Perhaps this parable was told in part to answer such questions. According to this parable, God's reign had in fact begun, but while the present age lasts, Satan does everything in his power to ruin God's salvatory plans. At the end of the age, however, God's kingdom would break forth in all its glory, and the rule of the evil one would come to an end. The parable has a strong eschatological emphasis and is designed to teach God's people to be patient, for the victory of God is beyond doubt, and will be celebrated in the world to come.

Let us begin by getting the parable before us. We will then turn to the interpretation given by Jesus. Finally we want to ask what might be some of the basic lessons that we are to learn from this parable story.

I. THE PARABLE (vv. 24-30)

"He put before them another parable" (v. 24). That kind of introductory formula is found nowhere else, except in verse 31, where it introduces the twin parables of the mustard seed and the leaven. Who the "them" are is not that clear, however, since Jesus and his disciples left the crowds and entered a house, after speaking in parables (v. 36), we assume that the "them" refers to the Galilean crowds that came to listen to Jesus. Having left the crowds, Jesus then led his disciples into a deeper understanding of the parable.

As we might expect from Matthew, this parable was spoken to illustrate some aspect of the "kingdom of heaven" (v. 24). Usually where Mark and Luke have kingdom of God, Matthew has kingdom of heaven, which would be understood by Jesus' contemporaries as meaning the same thing. "Heaven" was a common surrogate for God in Judaism, since it was thought inappropriate to mention the holy name "God" too often. The kingdom of heaven, said Jesus, could be compared to what the farmer in this parable did: he sowed good seed on his field in the hope of a good harvest.

"But while everybody was asleep, an enemy came and sowed weeds among the wheat, and then went away" (v. 25). There is no blame attached to the fact that the farmer, his workers, or anyone else slept. That's simply the backdrop for the story. We do not know who this enemy was, or what had created such animosity between him and this farmer, that he would do such dastardly thing: ruin the farmer's crop. That people got even with each other in this strange manner in the first century is well known. Gustav Dalman, who spent many years in the Palestine, tells of a farmer who got even with his neighbor who had let his cattle graze on his field, by sowing weed seed on his neighbor's land. This manner of seeking revenge was punishable under Roman law. This was, then, not an imaginary act, but a real life situation.

The enemy in our parable is not identified. But he comes at night, when family and hired men and women are asleep, with a bag of weed seed, and scatters this noxious seed on the field on which the farmer had already seeded wheat. Precisely what kind of weed seed he scattered on his field is not known. The Greek word ***zizanon*** is usually rendered as "darnel" in the English versions, a grass like chess or ryegrass, which in the early stages of its growth cannot be distinguished from wheat plants.

A light infestation of darnel could have been tackled by careful weeding, but a heavy infestation, such as we have in our parable, would not make selective weeding possible. "So when the plants came up and bore grain, then the weeds appeared also" (v. 26). The wheat plants would be hard to distinguish from the weed plants until both were in head. Therefore, the suggestion of the well-meaning servants of this householder, to pluck up the weed plants, did not seem feasible. The servants are in fact surprised to find weed plants among the wheat, for they know that their master had planted good seed (v. 27). But the farmer seems to know that his enemy has done this wicked deed (v. 28). "Some blackguard has done this to spite me," he explains (according to J. B. Phillips).

We would have expected the master to say Yes, go to it, and pull up the weeds. But he says No, for in plucking up the weeds they would also pluck up the wheat plants, and that would ruin the entire crop. The master's resolution is: "Let them both grow together until the harvest; and at harvest time I will tell the reapers, Gather the weeds first and bind them in bundles to be burned, but gather the wheat into my barn" (v. 30). The weed seeds could not be used for food, and would have to be separated from the grain at harvest time. Some interpreters suggest that the weed and wheat stalks would be cut with a sickle at harvest time; the wheat would be threshed and the darnel would be bound in bundles to be used for fuel. Since there was always a shortage of fuel in ancient Israel, there is nothing unusual about tying the cut weed-stalks into bundles and storing them for fuel. The wheat would be put into storage rooms and used for making bread flour. Others think that both wheat and weed stalks would be cut and threshed, and then the grains would be separated. (I have seen women in India sitting daily before a pile of rice and picking out the weed seeds, the dirt and the little stones from the rice.). Whether the stalks with the ripe ears were separated when the harvesters cut them with their sickles, or whether the grains, which were of a different color, were separated after the threshing, does not really change the meaning of the parable. It is to the meaning that we now turn. In this case, we must take Jesus' interpretation, given in verses 36 to 43 into account.

II. THE INTERPRETATION (vv. 36-43)

"Then he left the crowds and went into the house. And his disciples came to him, saying, Explain to us the parable of the weeds in the field" (v. 36). Whose house Jesus entered is not known, but it could well be that of Peter and Andrew, who had a house in Capernaum. It was in this house that Jesus, on an earlier occasion, had healed Peter's mother in law who lay ill with fever (Mt 8:14,15).

The explanation which Jesus gives to his disciples has allegorical elements and for that reason some scholars think that this interpretation could not have come from Jesus' mouth. But there is no reason to doubt the genuineness of Jesus' interpretation; the Hebrew word for parable (***mashal***) can include allegory. Besides, Jesus did not interpret all the details of this parable, but only those which are relevant to the basic thrust of the parable. For example, Jesus did not say who the servants who slept were. A Spanish Jesuit in the 16th century suggested that they were the bishops of the church, and that got him into deep trouble with Roman Catholic hierarchy.

The one who sowed the good seed, said Jesus, was "the Son of Man." This is the most common self-designation of Jesus. So we know who the sower in this parable, when it was first told, is. He sows good seed.

The field on which he sows is "the world" (***kosmos***), understood in our parable in its anthropological sense, meaning, the people of this world. That Christ sows good seed among the people of this world, may point to the world-wide mission of the church to spread the gospel. But, in contrast to the parable of the four soils, where the seed is identified as "the word" of the kingdom (Mt 13:19), here the seed is said to be "the sons of the kingdom." That's a Semitic idiom for people who belong to Christ's kingdom, who acknowledge his reign in their lives. They are sons (and daughters) who have accepted Jesus' message of the kingdom, and have entered into it.

That they were sown by the divine Sower (Mt 13:38) may signify, that they are his children by grace. And, as children of Christ's kingdom, they have God for their Father (v. 43); they comprise a new family, united by faith with Christ and his Father. They live godly lives, and therefore are called "righteous" (v. 32). And some day they will shine in the kingdom of their Father (Dan 12:2,3).

By contrast, the weeds represent the children of the evil one, i.e., the devil. That's rather strong language for unbelievers. But unbelievers are under the power of the devil (see John 8:44, where Jesus calls his unbelieving opponents "children of the devil"). They are called "evil doers" in verse 41. The enemy who sowed them is the devil (v. 39). Matthew uses the Greek word for "devil" (***diabolos***), instead of the Hebrew "Satan." The two groups are set off from each other in radical fashion, even though in everyday life they live together. Here we can feel the tension that exists between God and the devil, who is bent on destroying God's saving purposes.

The children of the devil have an awful destiny. At the end of the age God will send out his angels who will reap the harvest of this earth. The end of the age is here called "the consummation" or "the wrap up" of the present age (***sunteileia*** in Greek; see also Mt. 24:3 and 28:20). The end of the age includes the judgment on the ungodly, and this judgment is often seen under the image of a harvest , both in the Old as well as in the New Testament (Joel 3:13; Jer 51:33; Hos 6:11; Rev

14:14-20). Those who are sent out to bring in the harvest of the earth are God's messengers, sent to do his bidding. And just as the weeds were collected for fuel, so the ungodly are gathered and thrown into the furnace of fire (v. 42), where there is weeping and gnashing of teeth. Weeping and gnashing of teeth describe both the pain and the rage, as well as the hopeless despair of the lost. In Matthew 8:12 this expression goes together with "darkness," which is another figure of speech for the place of the lost. No doubt this language is highly pictorial, however, judgment is a serious theme in the New Testament. It is the other side of grace. And lest anyone should think that the God of the Bible is only a God of wrath, as Marcion in the 2nd century taught, and Jesus is a God of love, we should notice that it is "the Son of Man," Jesus, who sends out the angels to gather the causes of sin and all evil doers for judgment (v. 41). The "causes of sin" (*skandalon*) may refer to those who draw others away from Christ. The parallel "and all who do evil" interprets "causes of sin." That they are gathered "out of his kingdom" does not mean that they were members of Christ's kingdom, but rather, they will have no place in the future kingdom, the kingdom of the Father (v. 43). They are cast into "the furnace of fire," which is elsewhere called *geena* (hell).

What is said here of the gathering of the evil ones is said also of the believers in Matthew 24:31: The Son of Man will send out his angels with a loud trumpet call, "and they will gather his elect from the four winds, from one end of heaven to the other." That is omitted in our parable. Here the focus is on the glorious future of the children of God. "The righteous will shine like the sun in the kingdom of their Father" (v. 43). Some of this language seems to come from Daniel 12:3, "And they that are wise shall shine as the brightness of the firmament and those who have taught many people what is right, will shine like the stars forever." The kingdom of the Father in verse 43 is the future heavenly kingdom into which God's children will enter at the end of the age.

Jesus rounds his interpretation of the parable off with the challenge:

"He who has ears, let him hear" (v. 43). He is not questioning whether or not people have ears. Rather, he means that people should pay attention to what Jesus is saying. We could translate the exhortation this way: "You have ears, don't you? then listen!"

We must now try to glean from the parable and its interpretation some truths that are applicable to our situation today.

III. THE APPLICATION

Let us begin by saying what the parable does not teach us! This parable has been used in the history of the church to illustrate the mixed character of the church, in which both true and false believers are members. But that would certainly not be Jesus' image of the church. Moreover, it is plainly stated, that the field is "the world." No apostolic writer imagines a church in which both believers and unbelievers are together in fellowship, and that we cannot know until the day of judgment who the true believers are. When infant baptism was introduced, perhaps as early as the 2nd century, the New Testament concept of a believers church became blurred. And when Constantine declared Christianity to be the state religion, more and more parents had their infants baptized, and the result was a kind of "mixed" character of the church. Out of this situation grew the concept of the "visible" and "invisible" church. The visible church was comprised of all those who were baptized, whether they had ever confessed their faith in Christ or not. From that dilemma arose the view that among this mass of so-called Christians, there were the genuine believers. God knew who they were, but it was not for others to say who was a genuine member of the body of Christ and who was not. That would become manifest only at the end of the age.

From this faulty understanding of the nature of the church, it followed, that it was not up to the church to discipline its members. "Let them both grow together until the time of the harvest." This was the position taken by the great 4th century theologian, Augustine. He warned against the practice of excommunicating members who evidently did not live as Christians are expected to live. Although rigorism in church life is not to be recommended, the apostles assume, that in a believers church, those who deny the Christian faith, either in word or deed, must be expelled, unless they repent (1 Cor 5:13). In the church there is forgiveness even for egregious sins, but forgiveness does not rule out discipline, as Jesus so clearly taught in Matthew 18:15-20. This parable really has nothing to do with church discipline, and so one should not use the words of the master to his servants, "Let them both grow together until the time of the harvest," to avoid all discipline.

What then does the parable say to us today? First, the disciples of Jesus are not called to carry out final judgment on evil doers. It is not our task to punish the wicked (and we are not speaking of the duties of a government to maintain law and order; see Romans 13). Our responsibility is, according to Paul, to "drive out the wicked person from among you," God will judge those on the outside" (1 Cor. 5:13). The church has not always observed this. One might think of the Crusades in the Middle Ages, the Inquisition, and other attempts to use external force to combat heresy or the infidel. That's why it is very wrong in our day for a believer to try to kill a doctor who performs abortions, much as we abhor the killing of infants in the womb. When on one occasion the Samaritans refused to offer Jesus and his disciples hospitality, James and John wanted to call down fire from heaven to destroy these inhospitable villagers. But

Jesus taught them otherwise (Lk 9:54). In some manuscripts, after this rebuke by Jesus, we have the following addition: "You do not know of what spirit you are, for the Son of Man has not come to destroy the lives of human beings but to save them."

The parable also teaches that God's wrath, which is revealed from heaven against all unrighteousness even now (Rom 1:16), will be manifest at the end of this age in the punishment of the wicked. The judgments of history are but forerunners of the final judgment. Here on earth much evil goes unpunished, and the good often goes unrewarded, but we can be sure that in the last judgment (Rev 6:12-17) there will be a deep division in humanity—the righteous will enter the eternal kingdom, and the ungodly will be the object of divine wrath.

And so we must be patient until that time comes. Here in this life believers live together with unbelievers; they love them and seek to win them for Christ. Until harvest time the two grow together. Although God has not revealed to us all the mysteries of his judgment of those who have never acknowledged his reign, we must take seriously the doctrine of final punishment.

From this parable we can also learn that there will be constant resistance by the devil and his hangers on, to the work of God and the people of God. We must take seriously what the New Testament says about demonic powers that oppose the church in its life and mission. However, the people of God do not despair because of that; they can resist the devil, because they know that he is essentially a defeated foe. His power was broken at the cross. And yet, as John puts it in Revelation 12:12, the devil knows that his time is short, and because of that he pursues the woman (the church) and makes war "with those who keep the commandments of God and hold the testimony of Jesus" (v. 17).

The inbreaking of the kingdom of God with the coming of Jesus did not immediately put an end to all the evil in this age. Until the devil is put away for good, he will continue to make war on the saints and seek to destroy God's work here on earth. In ***A Theology of the New Testament*** George Ladd writes: "The meaning of the parable is clear when interpreted in terms of the mystery of the kingdom: its present but secret working in the world. The kingdom has come into history but in such a way that society is not disrupted. The sons of the kingdom have received God's reign and entered into its blessings. Yet they must continue to live in this age, intermingled with the wicked in a mixed society." Only in the eschatological coming of the kingdom will the separation of the godly and ungodly be carried out.

Although believers support all worthy causes in the world in which they live, and pray that righteousness might prevail in our pagan society, they must be realistic and recognize that our present age is under the influence of the god of this age, Satan. And so when evil seems to triumph, they do not despair, because they know that they are on the winning side in the end. The kingdom of God is a present reality, but we still keep on praying, "Your kingdom come." And in God's good time it will come, and come it will in a most glorious manner, and God will be all in all.

CHAPTER SEVEN

THE RICH MAN AND LAZARUS
Luke 16:19-31

This woodcut is by an anonymous artist from Christoph Wiegel's **Biblia Ectypa: Bildnesse auss Heiliger Schrift, Alt und Neuen Testament** published in 1695.

THE RICH MAN AND LAZARUS   Luke 16:19-31

This story, like a number of others in the Gospels, does not have the word "parable" in it. However, whenever Jesus told a story which conveyed significant spiritual truths about the kingdom of God, we have a parable. Some expositors prefer to call them "example stories," but that doesn't change the meaning. And so we can legitimately call this "The Parable of the Rich Man and Lazarus."

Whether Jesus used a well-known story as his model and adapted it, is not certain. There is an Egyptian story, in which a rich man is given a very lavish funeral, while a poor man is buried very simply. The god of the dead then takes the story-teller into the underworld, the abode of the dead, and shows him that in the next world, the roles of these two men were reversed. The story appears in several different forms in Jewish folklore. In one version, a rich publican, by the name of Bar Ma'jan and a poor scholar both die. Bar Ma'jan had an elaborate funeral; the poor scholar a very simple one. Then a friend of the scholar has a dream, and in his dream he sees the poor scholar in the gardens of paradise beside a fresh stream of water, while the rich publican stands by the bank of the river, unable to reach the water.

If Jesus did make use of such popular stories, then he certainly put his own stamp on the material, and for two thousand years by now, the church has read this parable as God's inspired word. This parable carries a powerful message both for the people of God and for unbelievers. It has a life-changing quality about it. This parable led the famous Dr. Albert Schweitzer to leave the comforts of Europe behind and to spend the rest of his life in the almost unbearable heat of the tropics. He was trained in philosophy; was widely known as a theologian; had written a very influential book, entitled in its English translation, ***In Search of the Historical Jesus.*** He was also an accomplished musician; in fact he was an authority on the music of J. S. Bach

Then one day this parable drove home to his heart the truth, that he was a rich man, feasting sumptuously at Europe's cultural tables, while Africa (poor Lazarus) lay on Europe's door-step. And so he signed up with the Paris Missionary Society. But first he took his medical training, and then, leaving all the material and cultural advantages of his native Alsace behind, spent the rest of his life in equatorial Africa.

That's just one illustration of the life-changing power of Jesus' parables. And so this morning we want to listen in on the parable as Jesus told it two thousand years ago. The story can be seen as unfolding in three stages: First, we have two men in life—a rich man and Lazarus; then we see them in death—both die; and thirdly, we have two men in dialogue with each other after they die. However, this dialogue is not between the rich man and Lazarus, but between the rich man and Abraham, the father of all believers.

I. TWO MEN IN LIFE (vv. 19-21)

A. The Rich Man (v. 19)

"There was a rich man who was dressed in purple and fine linen and who feasted sumptuously every day." The parable is introduced in a very similar manner as the parable of the unjust steward (Lk 16:1-13): "There was a rich man." We don't know his name, although in English speaking countries he is sometimes called Dives, as if that were his name. But ***dives*** is simply the Latin word for "rich," an adjective, not a proper noun. There is a New Testament papyrus in the Bodmer library, in Geneva, which gives him the name that resembles the word Nineveh. And that is in fact the name he has in the Sahidic version, one of the early translations of the Greek New Testament into an Egyptian dialect. Evidently those who copied and translated the books of the Greek New Testament, felt the need to give him a name. But our Greek text has simply, "There was a rich man."

Imagine, if you had been asked to prepare a eulogy for this man's funeral, and you could think of nothing else, except that he was a rich man. You could readily give the dates of his birth and of his death; you could perhaps mention the names of his wife and children. But beyond that you couldn't think of anything else to say, except: he was a rich man. You wish you could say that he had been a loving husband, a good father to his children, a friendly neighbor, a helper of those in need. But no, all you can think of is: he was a rich man. Well, we do know a few things about him, but they are the kind of things one wouldn't want to say too much about at his memorial service.

We are told that he dressed and ate well. "He dressed in purple." To dress in purple means that he wore expensive clothes, clothes made of cloth that was dyed with a purple dye that came from a particular kind of shell fish. Purple was the color of royalty. Purple is probably a reference to his outer garments. The fine linen that he wore is a reference to costly undergarments. Egypt was the source of fine linen in those days.

Not only did he dress well; he also ate well: "He feasted sumptuously every day." Not only did he himself enjoy rich gastronomic fare, but no doubt he prepared lavish banquets to which he invited his friends. The word "daily" has suggested to some Bible students that, although he was a Jew, he even disregarded the sacred Sabbath law, in order to enjoy himself to the full.

The picture we get with this brief thumbnail sketch, is that of a hedonistic person, completely caught up in a steady stream of feasting. Enslaved to his selfish ways, he has no time to reflect on the meaning or purpose of life. Perhaps by living at such a maddening pace, he was spared the pain of thinking about the day when it would all be over, and he would have to stand before the Judge of all the earth.

The story is told of Louis XIV, 16th century king of France, that he prepared a splendid banquet for all the high and mighty of his kingdom. It was to be a glittering event. As the guests gathered, the king asked one of his courtiers, whether anything was missing. The perceptive man thought for a moment, and then replied with one word: "Permanence."

No doubt the lavish lifestyle that the rich man in our parable enjoyed, which he must have felt was his right to enjoy, made him blind for the needs of others. He had no eyes to look at Lazarus on his door step. Perhaps because he was wealthy he thought that he was in fact the object of divine blessing. According to the Old Testament law of retribution, as this was generally understood, if a person did right, he or she could be sure of material blessings, and if a person was poor, that was a sign that something was wrong in his or her life. This simple equation was exposed as inadequate in the Book of Job, for example, where a godly man lost all his material possessions. In fact the friends of Job were sure that he had sinned, else God would not be punishing him. But in the end they were shown to be wrong. Bad things happen to good people, too. But now let us look at the poor man!

B. The Poor Man (vv. 20,21)

"And at his gate lay a poor man named Lazarus, covered with sores, who longed to satisfy his hunger with what fell from the rich man's table; even the dogs would come and lick his sores."

Lazarus is the only person in all the parables of Jesus that is given a name, although some scholars think it was a symbolical name. The name may be derived from the Hebrew *el'azar*. "*El*" is the Hebrew generic word for god, and "*azar*" is the word to help. God is my helper, or God has helped. This was the name of Abraham's servant, Eleazar. It may simply be symbolic of those who put their trust in God who is their Helper. There is, however, another possible etymology of the word "Lazarus," and that is the Hebrew *lo'azar*, which would mean no helper, no one helps. But that explanation is less likely than the previous one.

How fitting that he should be called Lazarus ("God has helped")! Neglected by the privileged of this world, he had nowhere else to look for help but to God. He is called a "poor man" (***ptochos*** in Greek can be translated as beggar," as the NIV and KJV have it). The word "poor" may also suggest his piety, for already in Old Testament times the word "poor" was sometimes used in that sense. We see it used that way by Jesus in Matthew 5:3, "Blessed are the poor in spirit" (Luke has simply, "Blessed are the poor"). They have nothing here on earth to depend on and have put their trust in God.

Lazarus was placed at the "door" of the rich man, according to some versions. But this should not be thought of as the door that led directly into the house. (In Greek the word for that door is ***thura,*** but in our parable we have the word ***pulon***, which may be translated "gate" rather than door (as NRSV has it). This was probably the gate that opened into the courtyard, suggesting that the rich man had a rather luxurious dwelling. We could perhaps also call it the vestibule, the foyer, the porch, the entrance.

Evidently Lazarus was unable to walk, for we are told that he was laid at the gate. Perhaps friends brought him there regularly in the hope that he might receive something from the table of the rich man. He "longed to satisfy his hunger with what fell from the rich man's table." The implication is, that his desire often went unsatisfied. In the KJV we read, that he longed for the "crumbs" that fell from the rich man's table, suggesting the rather untidy eating habits of the rich man's family. But the better manuscripts don't have "crumbs"; they read simply "that which fell from the rich man's table." Very likely that refers to the crusts of bread with which people wiped their greasy fingers with which they ate. Such crusts were the ancient equivalent of napkins or serviettes on our tables.

In any case, Lazarus hoped that he would get some of the leftovers from the rich man's table. A few manuscripts add, "but no one gave him anything." That is probably a carryover from Luke 15:16, where that is said of the prodigal son's food. We should not imagine Lazarus as lying under the table of the rich man, waiting for crumbs to fall from the table. He was kept well out of sight and would probably have depended on some kind servant to bring him the leftovers.

Not only was Lazarus destitute and crippled, but he was also diseased. He was covered with sores, ulcers. And as he lay there, the pariah dogs came round to get a share of the leftovers. These scavengers licked his sores, not because they were kinder than human beings, but because he could not drive them away. Dogs were considered to be the epitome of uncleanness in Israel, and their presence would have been very embarrassing for Lazarus. What an unspeakably sad and hopeless condition this poor man was in! And with that we come to the second stage of our story. Like all human beings, both men eventually die. The order in which the deaths of the two men is mentioned, is now reversed. Lazarus dies first.

II. TWO MEN IN DEATH (vv. 22, 23)

A. The Poor Man (v. 22)

"The poor man died and was carried away by the angels to the bosom of Abraham." Nothing is said of his funeral. Nothing is said of his burial either. Not to receive a proper burial was considered to be an awful tragedy in ancient Israel. We have to assume that his relatives or friends buried him, but that is left unsaid.

More significant than his funeral is the comment, that the angels came and carried him away. That's a very tender and beautiful touch. God sends his heavenly messengers to bring Lazarus home to the place of heavenly bliss. Here he is united with the father of all believers, Abraham. The angels carry Lazarus to the "bosom" of Abraham. That word (Greek: ***kolpos***) is a very Semitic expression. It can mean the breast, or the loose fold of a person's garments, or even lap. Luther in his translation took it to mean "lap" (***Schoss***). I must say, that the prospect of sitting on Abraham's lap some day has never attracted me very much. But there is another meaning of this word in the New Testament. It is said of John, the apostle, that he lay at the bosom (***kolpos***) of Jesus at the last supper (Jn 13:23).

We probably do best if we combine several aspects of this imagery. It's a pictorial expression to indicate the loving relationship between people, but also, it is the place of honor at the banquet table. The world to come was often thought of in terms of sitting at table with Abraham, Isaac and Jacob in the coming kingdom. Jesus said, he would not drink of the fruit of the vine until he drank it anew in his Father's kingdom. To sit or lie next to someone at table speaks also of friendship, fellowship, and honor. Perhaps there is a deliberate contrast here between the leftovers that Lazarus had to content himself with, when he was on earth, and the rich banquet table in the heavenly world, seated next to the father of the faithful, Abraham.

We should, of course, not try to draw a complete picture of heaven on the basis of one figure of speech in a parable. We have an array of images of heaven in the New Testament. One might mention the Father's house with many rooms, the building made without hands, eternal in the heavens, the city of gold, the new Jerusalem, and in the parable at the beginning of Luke 16, there is a reference to the eternal tents. But now we must turn to the darker side of what happened in our parable. The rich man also died.

B. The Rich Man

"The rich man also died and was buried." And what Paul wrote in his letter to Timothy, proved to be true in this rich man's case as well: "We brought nothing into this world and we will carry nothing out" (1 Tim 6:7). I heard of relatives of a wealthy uncle, who could hardly wait until he died, hoping that they would inherit a share of his wealth. So when they heard that he had passed away, they immediately phoned his attorney to ask, how much he had left. The lawyer, somewhat upset by this shameful manifestation of greed, replied rather curtly, "everything." Yes, this rich man also left everything behind.

Whereas there was no mention made of Lazarus's burial, the rich man's burial is carefully noted. "The rich man also died and he was buried." One can only imagine what his funeral must have been like. The body would have been washed and perfumed and wrapped in a shroud, as was the custom at that time. Professional mourners and musicians might be hired. The whole village would accompany the bier on which the body lay to the graveyard. We don't know what was said at the funeral, but when this man awoke in the next world, he was in terrible torment. He had gone to Hades. That word means literally "the unseen world," and can be used for the abode of the dead. In ancient Greek mythology, Hades was the name of the god of the underworld.

In the Old Testament the abode of the dead is called "*Sheol*"—the equivalent of the Greek *Hades*. However, in our parable Hades is not simply the abode of the dead, but a place of torment. Although it may not be wise to translate Hades as "hell," it looks as if Hades in our parable comes close to the word for hell (*geena*) used in the New Testament. Some scholars suggest that we should think of Hades in our parable as representing the intermediate state (ie., between death and the final judgment), but I am not sure that is very helpful.

Professor David Wenham of Oxford suggests: "It should be understood as pictorial rather than as anything like a literal description of... hell." He would say the same for the state of bliss in which Lazarus found himself after death. When we get to heaven we do not expect to carry on a conversation with people who are in hell, as happens in this parable. Although this parable does not, in the words of A. M. Hunter of Aberdeen, "tell us about the furniture of heaven or the temperature of hell," it does make plain that there will be a division of humankind after death, and that the righteous will enter a state of bliss and the unrighteous a place of torment. That's a rather offensive teaching in our society today. But we should remember, that the kindest person that ever lived, our Lord Jesus, said that in the last day, when the dead rise from their graves, "those who have done good will rise to the resurrection of life, and those who have done evil, to the resurrection of condemnation" (Jn 5:29). The kindest mouth that ever spoke, said that in the last judgment some would be set to the right and some to the left (Mt 25: 33).

The rich man in our parable went to Hades, and there he looks up and sees Abraham far away, and Lazarus at his side. And that sets the stage for the dialogue between two men in the other world. The dialogue, however, is not between the rich man and Lazarus, but between the rich man and Abraham. Lazarus never speaks a word in this parable. While on earth he put his trust in God, and bore his tragic lot quietly. We don't hear him complain. There are no expressions of bitterness. He never murmurs against the way God seems to have distributed wealth in this world; nor does he rail against the rich. He is simply silent.

III. THE DIALOGUE BETWEEN TWO MEN (vv. 24-31)

A. The Address (v. 24a)

Seeing Abraham, the rich man calls out, "Father Abraham." He must have thought, someone made a terrible mistake, for a child of Abraham was not supposed to go to the place of torment. According to the teaching of some rabbis, Abraham had earned extra merits before God by his complete obedience, and so if a son of Abraham came up short in the end, the merits of Abraham should really cover him. Some rabbis even suggested, that God would place an angel at the mouth of **Gehenna** (hell), to make sure that no circumcised Israelite would ever enter that terrible place.

Be that as it may, it will soon become obvious, that this man had no right to claim Abraham as his father. He wasn't a true child of Abraham at all, even though he was a Jew. Already some Old Testament prophets had made it plain, that without the circumcision of the ear, and the heart, there was no advantage before God in having the outward seal of the covenant, the circumcision of the flesh.

When Israel became apostate, Hosea was to give the name *"Lo Ammi"* to one of his sons, which means "you are not my people." A true Jew, writes Paul to the Romans, is not one who is a Jew outwardly, but one who is a Jew inwardly, who is a true believer, a true son of Abraham (Rom 2:29). In that respect the apostle Paul simply followed in the steps of Jesus and the prophets. In a controversy with Jesus, the unbelieving Jews of his day claimed, "Abraham is our father" (Jn 8:33). Jesus then asks them why they wanted to kill him. Abraham did no such outrageous thing. Clearly they were then not children of Abraham. Rather, they were children of the devil, for he is a murderer. Similarly the claim of the rich man in Hades, that he was a son of Abraham, falls to the ground. He had demonstrated by the way he lived on earth, that Abraham was not his father.

B. The Petition (v. 24b)

In his distress the rich man cries for mercy. He begs Abraham, "Send Lazarus to dip the tip of his finger in water and cool my tongue; for I am in agony in these flames."

In Jewish thought, paradise was a place of springs of water, and that is also how John in the last chapter of the Bible describes the restored heavenly paradise. He sees a river flowing from the throne of God with fruit trees flourishing on its banks. Hades, by contrast, is without water. On earth the rich man had been independent. He had money; he could buy whatever struck his fancy. But now he needs help. On earth he never moved a finger to help Lazarus. Now he wants Lazarus to dip his finger in water and cool his tongue.

Lazarus is still someone he thinks he can order around. "Send him over here," he says. The fact that he knows the beggar's name suggests that he knew who the poor fellow, who used to lie at his gate, was.

C. The Reply (vv. 25,26)

Abraham answers tenderly. He calls him "child" (***teknon*** -a caritative, an endearment word). "Remember that during your lifetime you received your good things, and Lazarus in like manner evil things; but now he is comforted here, and you are in agony. Besides all this, between you and us, a great chasm has been fixed, so that those who might want to pass from here to you, cannot do so, and no one can cross from there to us."

Abraham reminds the rich man that he has received in full (apolambano) "his good things in life." Lazarus has received not "his evil things" but just "evil things," for he did not deserve them. God was not punishing him because of sins committed. He suffered innocently. The rich man, however, had regarded his wealth as "his" good things. And so while Lazarus is now comforted, he is tormented.

Not only is help for the rich man unavailable; it is impossible to give. There is a great chasm that has been "fixed" and so there is no way anyone can cross over from one place to the next. There is no purgatory from which it is possible to escape by prayers and offerings. There will be no reversal of his fate. His eternal destiny has been sealed.

D. The Concern (vv. 27,28)

Having realized that his own situation is hopeless, the rich man now expresses concern for his relatives. He has five brothers who evidently are living the way he had lived, and he's afraid that they might end up in the same awful place. For the first time in this parable he expresses concern for others. He asks Abraham to send Lazarus back to his father's house to warn his brothers, lest they too land in Hades. That's the second time in this story that he asks Abraham to send Lazarus on a mission. Somehow he thinks he can still treat Lazarus as if he were of no account. He can be pushed around, ordered about, like a messenger boy.

Harsh though it may seem, his request is turned down. The reason is a very simple one: it wouldn't do any good. That people are capable of disbelief in the face of convincing evidence for faith, is something we can see all around us today. It was so even in Jesus' day. The signs which Jesus did had no effect on the stubborn unbelief of his opponents, the religious hierarchy. Jesus' resurrection should have convinced his contemporaries that he was God's Messiah, but they persisted in unbelief.

E. The Explanation (vv 29-31)

Abraham now explains that there is no need to send Lazarus, because his brothers have "the law and the prophets." That's one way the Jews sometimes spoke of their Bible; we call it the Old Testament. In other words, if they have the Bible, they know what to do to avoid ending up where the rich man now found himself. All they needed to do, was to listen to the Bible and to do what it says, and they will also arrive at the bosom of Abraham when life comes to an end.

The rich man, however, finds Abraham's explanation unacceptable. "No! father Abraham, but if someone from the dead goes to them they will repent." He knows that his brothers aren't listening to the law and the prophets; he hadn't either. And he is sure that, if in a miraculous fashion someone should return from the world of the dead and warn them, they would listen and repent. Notice, he sees now that they did need to repent, if they wanted to go to Abraham's bosom. Evidently they were living the same kind of selfish life he himself used to live.

The law and the prophets had been available to the rich man when he was on earth. If he didn't own a Bible, he could hear the Scriptures read in the synagogues, not only on the Sabbath, but also on Tuesdays and Thursdays, for no Jew was to be deprived of the word of God for longer than three days.

Abraham then closes off the dialogue with a very incisive explanation, as to why sending Lazarus to witness to his brothers would not do any good. "If they did not listen to Moses and the prophets, neither will they be convinced, even if someone rises from the dead." Well then, what did Moses and the prophets say? Moses has a lot to say about the treatment of the poor (e.g., Deut 24). Israel was not to take advantage of them, but pay them wages; leave something in the fields for them to glean; make sure that they were treated fairly, and so forth.

And what about the prophets? Let me give only one excerpt from Isaiah 58:10: "If you offer your food to the hungry and satisfy the needs of the afflicted, then your light will shine in the darkness and your gloom like the noonday." So, Moses and the prophets are clear; a genuine faith manifests itself in helping the needy. But that is something the rich man had not done, and his brothers were following in his footsteps. They were not listening to Moses and the prophets, and so they would not be converted by a miracle either. Jesus had done many miracles. He had in fact raised the poor man's namesake, Lazarus, the brother of Martha and Mary, from the dead. Did that lead the Jewish leaders to faith? No. We are told in John 12:9,10, that Jesus' enemies planned to put Lazarus to death, because some of the Jews were going over to Jesus.

James Denney, a Scottish New Testament scholar of a former generation, in commenting on this parable, makes this observation: "If people can be inhuman with the Bible in their hands, and Lazarus at their gate, no revelations of the splendours of heaven or the anguish of hell will ever make them anything else."

And so the curtain falls; the parable stops abruptly. Nothing more needs to be said. The hearers in Jesus' day, and we today, are simply left stunned, pricked in our consciences. And we ask ourselves: what is this parable telling me? Let me offer a few suggestions in conclusion.

CONCLUSION:

A. What the parable does not teach:

1. Let me begin by saying, that it does not teach that the possession of material goods as such is wrong. They are also gifts from God, assuming, of course, that they have been honestly acquired. This man was not lost because he was wealthy. Abraham also was wealthy. And the poor man was not saved because he was poor. The parable overturns Jewish conventional wisdom which saw the rich as people blessed by God and the poor as suffering because of some misdeed.

2. Secondly, as far as we know, this man was not lost because of gross crimes he had committed. It is not said that he lived an immoral life, or that he was a

thief, or even that he kicked Lazarus, or beat his wife, or something like that. It wasn't what he had done, but rather what he had not done, that got him into Hades; it was because of something he neglected, that plunged him into outer darkness. He simply did not notice Lazarus at his gate, and couldn't have cared less.

3. Thirdly, the parable does not give us detailed information on the life to come. Nothing is said about the resurrection from the dead, of Christ's appearing, of God's judgment seat, and so forth. If I may quote from Professor Wenham's book on parables once more, he writes: "The parable was not intended as a map of the afterlife, though it has often been used or misused in that way. But it was meant to make some very clear points about getting into the coming feast of the kingdom of God or rather about the dangers of not getting in, and about the fearfulness and irrevocability of judgment."

B. What then does the parable teach?

1. Clearly it teaches, that our eternal destiny is determined by the decisions we make here in life. Once life is over, it is too late to change our destiny. How God will judge the many who have never heard the gospel, we leave to a righteous and merciful God, but the Bible holds out no hope for those who deliberately refuse God's gracious offer of eternal life.

2. The parable also teaches, that true children of Abraham (and that includes all Christian believers) listen to what the Scriptures have to say. And those who have put their faith in Christ will demonstrate their faith in works of love and mercy. There is no suggestion in this parable that salvation can be earned by good works. But a faith, as the apostles James puts it, without works is dead (Jam 2:17). Or, in the words of Paul, we have been saved by grace not by works, but we have also been created in Christ Jesus unto good works (Eph 2:9,10).

3. Earthly things never become part of our personality; we leave them all behind when we die. But good deeds, done in the name of Christ, even giving the proverbial cup of water, are far too valuable to be left behind. The Seer of Patmos heard a voice from heaven which said: "Blessed are the dead who from now on die in the Lord. Yes, says the Spirit, they rest from their labors." This beatitude is then followed up with an important comment: "For their works go with them" (Rev 14:13). Good deeds that spring from our faith in God are far too precious to be left behind. Our parable challenges us to be good stewards of God's gifts here on earth.

Dr. Helmut Thielicke, German preacher and theologian, whose books are read the world over, some years ago published a book of sermons on the parables of Jesus. And in his exposition of the parable of the rich man and Lazarus he makes the comment: "Our pocket books may have more to do with heaven and hell, than our hymn books."

I close with the words of Menno Simons: "True evangelical faith cannot lie dormant, it clothes the naked, it feeds the hungry, it comforts the sorrowful, it shelters the destitute, it serves those that harm it, it binds up that which is wounded, it has become all things to all people."

CHAPTER EIGHT

THE FRIEND AT MIDNIGHT Luke 11:5-13

This is a transparency, collodion on a glass slide
from the late 1800's, courtesy of the
George Eastman House Still Photograph Archive.

THE FRIEND AT MIDNIGHT Luke 11:5-13

The evangelist Luke has much to say about prayer. Chapter 11 begins with Jesus himself at prayer (v. 1). After finishing his prayer, his disciples came to him and asked him to teach them to pray. This is the only place in the Gospels in which the disciples ask Jesus to teach them. By now they were becoming conscious of their apostolic calling, and although they were familiar with the Jewish prayer practices, they wanted Jesus to show them how disciples of Jesus should pray. Other Jewish groups, including the disciples of John, also had their distinctive prayers.

Jesus responds to their request by giving them a model prayer. In English it has become known as the "Lord's Prayer," but it is a prayer that our Lord could not have prayed in its entirety. The prayer includes a request for the forgiveness of sins, and our Lord was sinless. But it is a model prayer for the followers of Jesus. In other languages it is often called simply the "Our Father." (In Latin it is the **pater noster**, in German "**das Vater Unser**.")

Following this model prayer, Luke attaches a short parable on prayer (vv. 5-11). The parable is unique to Luke's Gospel. In just a few colorful words Jesus describes a true to life situation which illustrates God's readiness to hear our prayers. Following the parable, he adds a few words of Jesus (vv. 12,13), designed to encourage his disciples to pray.

We want to begin with an expansion of this rather brief parable. Next, we must ask ourselves what the parable teaches us about prayer. Finally, taking account of the words of Jesus in verses 12 and 13, we want to listen to our Lord's encouragement to pray.

I. THE PARABLE OF THE FRIEND AT MIDNIGHT

This parable has had a number of titles given to it; some of them a bit opprobrious: "The Disobliging Neighbor," "The Grumpy Neighbor," and others. However, there seems to be a greater emphasis on friendship than on grumpiness in this story, and so we will retain the title: "The Friend at Midnight."

The parable begins with a question; in fact it seems as if the entire parable story is in question form: "Which one of you?" The effect is that it addresses the hearers personally and forces them to make a decision about what Jesus is about to tell them. Also, it assumes that the hearers know that such things happened in their lives, and from such an "earthly" event Jesus will teach them an important spiritual truth.

Jesus challenges his hearers to imagine the following situation: "Suppose one of you has a friend, and you go to him at midnight and say to him, 'Friend, lend me three loaves of bread; for a friend of mine has arrived and I have nothing to set before him" (v. 6). That's not yet the whole story, but let us stop for a moment and describe the situation. The picture is that of neighbors in a Galilean village who are friends. One of them unexpectedly receives a guest at midnight. No doubt he was a traveler and not a resident. Travel at night was not uncommon in those days. The wise men traveled at night, as did the holy family (Mt 2:9,14). The reason evidently was to avoid the heat of the day.

Tired and hungry this traveler comes to a village at midnight and expects a friend to provide him with hospitality. But, because he came at such an unusual hour, he placed his host in a predicament. Either he must let the night visitor go hungry, something not done in that culture, or he must go to a sleeping neighbor friend and try to borrow some bread. Refusing to feed a guest, would mean to violate a fundamental law of hospitality. But, rousing a neighbor at midnight could strain his friendship to the breaking point. Shops were closed by midnight in small villages. Besides, one didn't normally buy bread in shops anyway, since bread was baked at home. Housewives baked frequently, often daily, and so this family had no extra loaves in the "deep freeze," as we might say.

No doubt the story so far brought smiles to Jesus' listeners, for it is so true to life, and all of them by now would be curious to know how the story ended. The host decides to go to his neighbor friend and borrow three loaves of bread. That would be standard fare for an evening meal. We shouldn't think in terms of loaves in our modem use of the word. Loaves in those days were often no bigger than a stone which one could hold in one hand. This is reflected in Jesus' comment: "Which of you if his son asks for bread, will give him a stone?" (Mt 7:9). Borrowing from a neighbor was common practice in those days. However, to wake up a family at midnight in order to borrow bread, was certainly out of the ordinary.

The host goes to his neighbor, awakens his friend, either by knocking on the door or by calling his name or by making noise. Knocking is not done in all societies, but it was well known in Israel. Houses in those days were relatively small, consisting as a rule of one room, used for sitting, dining, and sleeping. Cooking was often done outside or under a lean-to. The houses of the common people had but one door and for night a wooden bar might be put across it from the inside for safety purposes. In any case, a locked door was not that easy to manipulate.

The sleeping householder hears his neighbor's voice and responds: "Do not bother me; the door has already been locked, and my children are with me in bed; I cannot get up and give you anything" (v. 7). People often slept on mats spread out and the whole family slept in one room. In such circumstances it was a bit complicated to get up and find something in the dark, unless one wanted to wake up the entire family. And so the disturbed neighbor friend asks not to be bothered. "I cannot get up" is the equivalent of "I don't want to get up." Apparently he would be happy to lend him a few loaves, but not go to the trouble of finding them, opening the door, and giving them to him. He knew that his friend, in return, would bring him three loaves next day, after the morning baking. So it wasn't that he was asked to "give" his neighbor three loaves, but simply to "lend" them.

The neighbor's response was far from pleasant. It was an all too human response of someone who is disturbed in his sleep. "Don't bother me!" However, he also realizes that his refusal would create bad feelings between him and his friend, if he didn't oblige. Friendship was highly valued in that culture. Friends were thought of as being in covenant with each other, and that meant they owed each other covenant responsibilities. He can't let his friend go home without bread. And that's where the story ends. We assume, from what Jesus says in verse 8, that the man did in fact get up and give his neighbor a few loaves. Let us now turn to Jesus' observation on what this man did in the end.

II. JESUS' OBSERVATION

"I tell you, even though he will not get up and give him anything because he is his friend, at least because of his persistence he will get up and give him whatever he needs" (v. 8).

Up until this point the parable was in the form of a rhetorical question. But now Jesus answers his own question. He seems to be saying that it's not simply because of friendship that he will get up and give his neighbor what he needs, but because of his persistence. And at this point we face a serious translation problem.

The Greek word, translated as "persistence" in some English versions, is ***aneideia***. This word occurs only here in the New Testament and so it is not surprising that translators have a problem with it. Etymologically the word means "no shame." Could it be that the man inside does not want to be put to shame, and so he gets up and gives his friend the loaves? The "his" then refers to the sleeping neighbor and not to the one knocking on his door. In other words, it's not because of the persistence, the impunity, the shamelessness of the friend who rouses his neighbor at midnight, but it is the sleeping neighbor who is concerned about the honor of his name. His sense of shame would drive him out of bed, even when his friendship would not. If we are right in the reading of the text this way, it is much easier to make the application of the parable to the prayers of God's children.

If one renders the word as "persistence," and applies it to the one knocking at the door, we run the risk of suggesting, that God is like this grumpy neighbor, who has to be badgered into action by our persistence. If, on the other hand, we take it in the sense of "shame," the implication would be that God's honor is at stake when his children pray. And so we can come to him with confidence, knowing that he is a generous giver of good gifts. We may have an illustration of this aspect of prayer in Exodus 32:12, where it is recorded that Moses, after the golden calf debacle, pleaded with God not to destroy Israel, for God's honor was at stake. What will the Egyptians say, argues Moses, when they hear that God delivered them out of Egypt, only to kill them in the desert? In other words, the Egyptians would lose respect for the God of Israel.

If, on the other hand, ***aneideia*** should have to be translated as "persistence," then the rule of contrast must be applied. That is, by teaching the lesser, it points to the greater. In other words, even this grumpy neighbor could not deny the request of his friend, when he persisted in asking for bread; then how much more willingly will God respond to the prayers of his children.

If a human friend can be induced to help a needy person out, much as he hates to, then imagine how God will respond when his children cry out to him. According to this interpretation God is much kinder than the unobliging neighbor. He is our Father and listens when his children pray. Jewish rabbis suggested that the angels in heaven were allowed to sing only at night; during the day they had to be silent so that God could hear the prayers of his children.

III. ENCOURAGEMENT TO PRAY

Whether the following sayings of Jesus were spoken on the same occasion as the parable of the friend at midnight, is not quite certain, since the same sayings are found in Matthew 7:7-11. We should, however, not rule out the possibility that Jesus spoke these same words in different contexts. The evangelist Luke has tied them closely to the parable.

A. The Exhortation (vv. 9,10)
"So I say to you, ask, and it will be given you; search, and you will find; knock, and the door will be opened for you. For everyone who searches finds, and for everyone who knocks, the door will be opened."

Here we have three verbs in the present imperative, which means that Jesus exhorts us to keep on asking, to keep on searching, and to keep on knocking. One might liken these imperatives to three hammer blows with which a nail is driven firmly into the wood. The three verbs should not be thought of as different ways of coming to God; they all speak of the same activity, namely of prayer. It is an example of synonymous parallelism.

It is possible, however, that the three verbs suggest different levels of intensity, beginning with the lesser (ask) and moving to the stronger verb (search), and finally to the verb "knock," indicating even greater intensity. Intensity should, however, not be understood in terms of louder or more often repeated prayer, but rather as ongoing. Persistent prayer should also not suggest that God is mean spirited, and that he has to be worn down until he finally yields to our request. It is pagan to think that God needs to be won over by our persistence; he is our Father, as the next verses show.

B. The Illustration (vv. 11-13)

"Is there anyone among you who, if your child asks for a fish, will give a snake instead of a fish? Or if the child asks for an egg, will give a scorpion? If you then, who are evil, know how to give good gifts to your children, how much more will the heavenly Father give the Holy Spirit to those who ask him?"

It would be cruel if a parent gave a hungry child a harmful substitute, such as a snake or scorpion, instead of a fish or an egg, not to mention the deception involved in such an offer. But if human parents would never treat their children in this manner, then surely God would never treat his children in that way. Human parents, Jesus adds, are sinful ("if you being evil"), but even sinful people can do good; they don't treat their children cruelly (at least not normally). When we make our requests known to our Father in heaven, we can be sure, that we are not praying to a reluctant God. He is willing, as Matthew has it, to give his children "good things." Luke states that he will give the Holy Spirit to those who ask. The Spirit is of course the source of all blessings in the life of disciples of Jesus, and the "good things" which Matthew mentions would be included in the gift of the Spirit.

The assurance that our prayers are heard by a gracious and generous Father, still leaves us with many unanswered questions about prayer. One of the questions is that of "unanswered" prayer. The apostle Paul prayed repeatedly, for God to remove the thorn from his flesh, but his request was not answered.

However, he received the assurance that God's grace was sufficient for his needs (2 Cor 12:8,9). One might also think of Jesus' prayer in Gethsemane, to let the cup pass by. That was not the Father's will and Jesus accepted that. "Not my will but yours be done," he said. In his high priestly prayer (John 17), he prayed that the church might be one, and that prayer, it seems, has not yet been completely answered. C. S. Lewis writes in his **Letters to Malcolm**, that "every war, every famine or plague, and almost every deathbed is a monument to a petition not granted."

In his book on parables, David Wenham writes, "The promise of answered prayer is not a blank cheque, guaranteeing that God will answer every prayer for a miracle, let alone prayers for the satisfaction of personal whims or desires. What it is, is a promise [of calling us] into a relationship with a Father who listens to his children, cares about their needs and loves to give them good things." In his book on prayer, the Norwegian O. Hallesby suggests, that if we have a spirit of prayer then we will "scarcely pass through an experience before we speak to God about it, either in supplication, in sighing, in pouring out our woes before him in fervent requests, in thanksgiving and adoration."

Fortunately we do not need to know the answer to all the mysteries of prayer in order to keep on praying. We have a wonderful promise in Romans 8:26,27, which assures us, that even though we do not really know what or how to pray, the Spirit takes our inner groanings and interprets them before God our heavenly Father. May God grant us a spirit of prayer!

CHAPTER NINE

THE PHARISEE AND THE TAX COLLECTOR
Luke 18:9-14

This woodcut is by an anonymous artist from Christoph Wiegel's **Biblia Ectypa: Bildnesse auss Heiliger Schrift, Alt und Neuen Testament** published in 1695.

THE PHARISEE AND THE TAX COLLECTOR
Luke 18:9-14

This parable follows immediately upon the parable of the widow and the unjust judge (Lk 18:1-8)—a parable that focuses on prayer. In the passage we are about to study today we are going to observe two men at prayer. Jesus lets us overhear the prayers of a Pharisee and a tax collector. But there is something in our parable that goes beyond the topic of prayer. In it we are confronted with the fundamental question of how a person can be saved, how one can enter the kingdom of God. The Pharisee stands in the presence of God in the temple, where it was thought prayer was particularly efficacious. He lists all his good deeds, but the tax collector casts himself on God's mercy. Jesus' verdict at the end of the parable (v. 14) makes it clear, that salvation is not by works but by grace.

The parable is addressed generally to people who "trusted in themselves that they were righteous and regarded others with contempt" (v. 9). The "others" would be fellow Jews who belonged to "the crowd, which does not know the law" (Jn 7:49). They were Jews who were indifferent to the many laws and regulations that had developed over the centuries regarding such matters as tithing, fasting, the Sabbath, and other areas of everyday life. The Pharisees went far beyond what the Old Testament required, and they were generally respected highly for their religious devotion. The last thing people listening to Jesus would have expected was that a Pharisee was not pleasing to God. Those of us who have heard and read the New Testament from childhood up, don't find this parable all that shocking, because we have been pre-conditioned to think negatively of Pharisees. But that was not the case with the original hearers of this parable.

Let us then go through this parable story and observe, first, the Pharisee at prayer (vv. 10-12); second, we want to listen to the tax collector's prayer (v. 13); finally we want to hear what Jesus, who knows the hearts of all humans, has to say about these two men (v. 14).

I. THE PHARISEE AT PRAYER (vv. 10-12)

"Two men went up to the temple to pray, one a Pharisee and the other a tax collector" (v. 10). Since Jerusalem with its temple was situated on a hill, the appropriate verb to visit this holy place for prayer was "to go up." Daily public prayers took place in the temple in the morning and in the afternoon, but individuals might also go into the temple at any time for private prayers. Passing through the outer court, Jewish men entered "the court of the Israelites." Here they would speak their prayers audibly; silent praying was not practiced generally.

Jesus portrays a Pharisee at his worst. We should not infer from this parable that all Pharisees were hypocrites. Jesus is no doubt overdrawing the picture, for there were those belonging to the Pharisaic sect who were genuinely devout. Our Lord is not dealing with Pharisees as a class, but with a particular Pharisee. To put the picture of this particular man in perspective, we should begin by saying something about Pharisees in general.

A. The Pharisees in General

The Pharisees, as a religious sect within Judaism, emerged in the 2nd century B.C. They were known for their fanatical loyalty to the law of God and the oral tradition, called "the tradition of the elders" in the New Testament. Their aim was to lay down rules for every area of daily life. Most of the scribes, mentioned in the Gospels, came from the Pharisaic party. Whereas the Sadducees dominated the temple cult, the Pharisees were more influential in the synagogues. The Pharisees commanded considerable respect from ordinary people, much more so than the aristocratic Sadducees. However, the Pharisees tended to be legalistic and had a tendency to make a show of their holiness. And that quite naturally led to a disdain for those who were less circumspect when it came to God's law, and the Pharisaic interpretation of that law. Our parable illustrates this rather negative trait.

B. The Pharisee in the Temple

"The Pharisee, standing by himself, was praying thus, 'God, I thank you that I am not like other people: thieves, rogues, adulterers, or even like this tax collector. I fast twice a week; I give a tenth of all my income'" (vv. 11,12).

The Pharisee stands praying. That was the normal posture in prayer in Jesus' day and does not suggest a pompous attitude. Some scholars suggest that he was "standing by himself," because he felt superior to other people and did not want to be part of the crowd in the temple, he thought he was too good for the rabble. In the Sermon on the mount (Mt 6:5f.) Jesus condemns those who pray to show off their religiosity, particularly when their prayers were said on street corners where people could see and hear them.

The Pharisee in our parable begins by thanking God, that he is not like other people: robbers, evil-doers, adulterers, and even like the tax collector standing near by. Ostensibly it is a prayer of thanksgiving, but in fact he is congratulating himself. It is interesting that the pronoun "I" occurs at least four times in this short prayer. He is completely smug and self-satisfied. One listens in vain for a confession of sins, or a word of intercession for others in this man's prayer. He is confident that he has fulfilled all the commandments. It was of course noble and commendable to abstain from the vices which he mentions, for they are all condemned in the Old Testament. But to boast in his own righteousness and to despise others, such as the tax-collector, was completely contrary to the spirit of the Scriptures.

The apostle Paul also was a Pharisee, and his assessment of his religious assets, after he became a Christian believer, was very different. He writes to the Philippians, listing his Jewish credentials: "If anyone else thinks he has reason for confidence in the flesh, I have more; circumcised on the eighth day; of the people of Israel, of the tribe of Benjamin, a Hebrew of Hebrews; in regard to the law, a Pharisee; as for zeal, persecuting the church; as for legalistic righteousness, faultless" (Phil 3:4-6). But then he says this of his past: that what was gain to him then, he now counts as loss.

The arrogance which the Pharisee in our parable displays in the presence of God was not at all that unusual. There is a prayer by Rabbi Nehunia in the Talmud (Berakhoth 28b) that goes like this: "I give thanks to Thee, O Lord my God, that Thou hast set my portion with those who sit in the Beth ha-Midrash [house of learning] and Thou hast not set my portion with those who sit in [street] corners, for I rise early and they rise early, but I rise early for a word of the Torah and they rise early for frivolous talk; I labor and they labor, but I labor and receive a reward and they labor and do not receive a reward; I run and they run, but I run to the life of the future world and they run to the pit of destruction."

After mentioning several vices from which he abstains, the Pharisee in our parable speaks of several religious practices in which he engages. He claims that he fasts twice a week. This was certainly a work of supererogation, for there was only one obligatory fast in Israel, and that was on the Day of Atonement. After their return from exile in Babylon, several other fasts came to be observed. But devout Jews fasted more often than the Law required. From extra-Biblical sources we know that the Pharisees preferred to fast on Mondays and Thursday. These were market days in the villages of Galilee, when people from the countryside brought and bought agricultural products. These days were then convenient for Pharisees to show off their religious devotion, by making them fast days. Of people who engaged in this kind of hypocritical fasting, Jesus says, that they "disfigure their faces so as to show others that they are fasting" (Mt 6:16). In a Christian document from the early 2nd century, called the ***Didache*** (the Teaching), believers are counseled not to fast on Mondays and Thursdays like the hypocrites. Rather they should fast on Wednesdays and Fridays. It was a way in which Christians set themselves off from Jewish legalism. (That Christians also were in danger of become legalistic, is well attested in the history of Christianity.)

The Pharisees also went beyond the Law in the matter of tithing. The Law did not prescribe the tithing of certain crops (Dt 14:22), but the Pharisees tithed even garden herbs (Lk 11:42). The Pharisees tithed everything they bought. (Some Rabbis boasted that even their donkeys tithed.) There was nothing wrong with the tithing of one's income. But to boast in being punctilious in one's religious practices and to despise others, violated the spirit of prayer. In fact, nothing that this Pharisee did or did not do was wrong. But his religion had turned into self-righteous humbug. Although he addressed God (however, only once), he really talked about himself And with that we now turn to the other chief character in this parable: a tax collector.

II. THE TAX COLLECTOR'S PRAYER (v. 13)

"But the tax collector, standing far off, would not even look up to heaven, but was beating his breast and saying, 'God, be merciful to me a sinner'." This man doesn't get as much space in the story as the Pharisee, because he has nothing to report that would commend him to God. The tax collector stands "far off." Does that mean he stood in the court of the Gentiles? In that case the Pharisee must have seen him as he came into the temple and probably glowered at him, thinking, what right has that wretch to be in the temple anyway? However, as a Jew he had the right to enter the court of the Israelites, and that seems to be the picture in this case. To better sense the sharp contrast between these two men, we should say something in general about taxes and their collectors.

A. Tax Collectors in General

The Jews had their own temple tax and other religious dues to pay. On top of these taxes the Romans taxed land and cattle, as well as trade and transport goods. What was particularly aggravating, was the head-tax, enforced through periodic censuses. Some scholars estimate that Jews in the days of Jesus had to pay as much as 40% of their income in taxes.

To collect these taxes, an elaborate civil service was instituted, and here the grievances were accentuated. The privilege of tax-collection went to the highest bidder, who then farmed the work out to subordinates. There is a reference to a "chief tax collector" in the next chapter (Lk 19: 1ff.), by the name of Zacchaeus, whose life was turned around when he met Jesus. He was probably responsible for the customs taxes in his region. The top men would be Romans; the lower ranks, those who made the actual contact with the people, were Jews. The temptation of these tax collectors was to make their occupation profitable for themselves. As long as they brought in the required tax, the higher officials didn't worry about how or how much was collected. And so the tax collectors demanded more than was required of the public, giving the word "tax collector" a bad name. Honest tax collectors were the exception. To be a tax collector and an extortioner came to mean more or less the same thing. When tax collectors asked John the Baptist what they should do to show their repentance, he told them, "Don't collect more than is legal" (Lk 3:12,13). Tax collectors were equated with "sinners" (Lk 15:1) and with "Gentiles" (Mt 18:17) as undesirables. Not only were they despised because they worked for the Romans (which made them unclean), but also because of their dishonesty and greed, and their disrespect for the Sabbath. In fact it was widely thought that they were beyond the pale of redemption, for even if they should repent, they were hardly able to make amends where they had defrauded people.

B. The Tax Collector at Prayer

This man comes into the temple fully conscious of the fact that he is a rotter. He doesn't have a leg to stand on before a holy God. Whether he had ever heard Jesus speak about the kingdom of God and how one could become a member of that kingdom, is not known. He is keenly aware of his sinfulness; "he didn't even dare to lift up his eyes." We might add, "let alone his hands." Looking up to heaven and holding up one's arms in prayer was the standard gesture in prayer, and we may assume that's what the Pharisee did. This gesture was taken over by the early church (1 Tim 2:8). The tax collector in our story may have been too embarrassed to attend the local synagogue, where everyone knew him, and so he comes into the temple with downcast eyes and beats his breast. The tense of the verb denotes continuous action: "he kept on beating his breast." The breast or the heart were thought of as the seat of sin, and so this was a gesture of contrition and remorse.

He breaks out in the words, "God be merciful to me the sinner." The verb ***hilaskomai*** can mean to be propitiated; in other words, "let your anger be removed." He wants to be forgiven. Perhaps he did not know what to say in the presence of God; words of praise, adoration and thanksgiving fail him. The burden of sin weighs heavy on his heart. All he can do is cry out to God for mercy, for forgiveness. He comes before God with empty hands; he has nothing to offer, no merits to claim, no excuses to make, no explanation for past failures. And he doesn't compare himself with other people. He casts himself on God's grace and prays that his wrath be turned away from him.

After this vivid thumbnail sketch of two men at prayer, Jesus pronounces his verdict on their prayers.

III. THE DIVINE VERDICT (v. 14)

"I say to you this man went down justified to his house rather than the other. For everyone who exalts himself shall be humbled, but he who humbles himself shall be exalted."

A. The Justification of the Tax Collector

"Justification" is one of the great Pauline words, found here in the mouth of Jesus. It does not mean that Jesus condoned the tax collector's past misdeeds; he knew very well that tax collectors, almost without exception, were engaged in fraud. Already the Old Testament condemned deception, extortion and robbery. "If anyone sins and is unfaithful to the Lord by deceiving his neighbor...he must return what he has stolen or taken by extortion, or what was entrusted to him, or the lost property he found, or whatever it was he swore falsely about. He must make restitution in full, add a fifth of the value to it and give it all to the owner of the day he presents his guilt offering" (Lev 6:2-5). When the tax collector, Zacchaeus, repented of his past misdeeds, he made this promise as a sign that he was entering God's kingdom: "Look, half of my possessions, Lord, I give to the poor, and if I have defrauded anyone of anything, I will pay back four times as much" (Lk 19:8,9). And Jesus responded: "Today is salvation come to this house, because this man, too, is a son of Abraham" (Lk 19:10). In our parable, to be justified is the equivalent of being saved. And to be a true son of

Abraham means to be a genuine believer.

To go home justified implies that God has pardoned his sins, and that he is now reckoned as righteous. The Pharisee, by contrast, was not accepted by God in spite of all his religiosity. Nothing more is said about this tax collector. No doubt, like Zacchaeus, he will have tried to make right the many wrongs he had committed against other people, at least as far as he could. However, that is not the basic thrust of the parable. The parable teaches us, that when people are conscious of their sin, and know that they have no standing before God on the basis of their own merits, and humbly confess their sin, they can be assured of God's forgiving grace. We have an outstanding example of what the grace of God can do in the life of a tax collector in the person of Levi (Matthew). One can imagine that the other disciples must have looked at Matthew to begin with some suspicion when he was called by Jesus to be one of the twelve apostles. But, like Zacchaeus, and like the tax collector in our parable, he was "justified by faith," to use a Pauline expression. It is interesting that Matthew in his Gospel gives the list of the twelve apostles and after his own name he adds "the tax collector" (Mt 10:3). Perhaps he wanted to witness to the grace of God who had saved "a wretch like me." Mark in his list of the twelve apostles does not mention this opprobrious background of Matthew (Mk 3:18). From the "justification" of the penitent tax collector and the arrogance of the Pharisee, Jesus makes another observation.

B. Pride Versus Humility in God's Governance

"For all who exalt themselves will be humbled, and all who humble themselves will be exalted" v. 14b)

This saying probably points to the final judgment, when those who have humbled themselves before God here in this life will be exalted, and those whose lives are characterized by pride and arrogance will be greatly humbled; for they will not enter the eternal kingdom. But his principle of divine governance is often foreshadowed here on earth. We have an outstanding example in Nebuchadnezzar. When he walked on the roof of his royal palace and proudly proclaimed, "is this not the magnificent Babylon which I have built...by my mighty power and for my glorious majesty?" he heard a voice from heaven: "O king Nebuchadnezzar, to you it is declared: the kingdom has departed from you...until you have learned that the Most High has sovereignty over the kingdom of mortals and gives it to whom he will" (Dan 4:30-32). This is but one biblical example of how God puts down the proud and raises up the humble.

In the book, ***How to Read the Bible for All its Worth***, Gordon Fee tells the story of a Sunday school teacher, who did a magnificent job in telling the children the story of the Pharisee and the tax collector, and applying the lessons of the story to everyday life. In conclusion the teacher asked the children to pray with him. Here's how he prayed: "Thank you Lord, that we are not like the Pharisee in this story." Dr. Fee writes, that he didn't know whether to cry or to laugh at such a prayer. But before we laugh too hard, he warns us not to thank God that we are not like this Sunday school teacher.

In his parables Jesus tends to be gentle with sinners who acknowledge their failures, and hard on the outwardly religious people. He ate with tax collectors and prostitutes, but denounced the scribes and the Pharisees. This was not because Jesus preferred sin to religion, or because he wanted to paint as black a picture of the religious hierarchy as possible. It was because religion can keep people from entering the kingdom of God. In his day it prevented the religious from responding to the gospel. Religious people can easily fall into the sin of pride, and those who do not recognize their own need for forgiveness, cannot enter the kingdom of God.

CHAPTER TEN

THE MUSTARD SEED AND THE LEAVEN
Mark 4:30-32. Matthew 13:31-33. Luke 13:18-21

This woodcut is by an anonymous artist from Desiderius
Erasmus' **Noui Testamenti aeditio postrema**
published in 1547.

THE MUSTARD SEED AND THE LEAVEN
Mark 4:30-32. Matthew 13:31-33. Luke 13:18-21

Jesus told these twin parables to indicate the huge difference between the kingdom Of God as it appeared in the days of Jesus and its glorious manifestation at the end of the age. The two parables teach essentially the same basic truth. If there is a difference between them, then perhaps the parable of the mustard seed speaks of the extensive growth of God's kingdom, whereas the parable of the leaven puts the emphasis on the internal dynamic of God's reign,

We want to begin by examining the parables themselves, to discover what their basic meaning might be. Also, we must look for some practical implications of these parables for the life of the church and the individual believer in today's world.

The parable of the mustard seed is one in a trilogy of "seed" parables. We began this volume with a study of the Sower and the Seed (chapter one), which is found in all three Synoptic Gospels. Mark has another seed parable, not found in Matthew or Luke, namely that of the seed growing secretly (Mk 4:26-29). All three Synoptic writers have the parable of the mustard seed. In the case of the Sower and the Seed we have the added element of hindrances to the growth and maturation of the seed. However, there is still an abundant harvest in the end. And that contrast between small beginnings and a glorious consummation is present in all three of the seed parables.

Let us now turn out attention to the parable of the mustard seed!

I. THE MUSTARD SEED

A. The Parable

Here is Matthew's version: "He put before them another parable; 'The kingdom of heaven is like a mustard seed that someone took and sowed in his field; it is the smallest of all seeds, but when it has grown it is the greatest of shrubs and becomes a tree, so that the birds of the air come and make nests in its branches'" (13:31,32).

The mustard seed was used in Jesus' day for seasoning and for medicinal purposes. Also, it served as food for doves and other fowl. According to Matthew it was planted in the field (Mark has "in the ground"), but Luke has "in the garden." It wasn't really the smallest of all seeds, but that's how it was thought of proverbially. Jesus often uses hyperbolic language to make the truth stick better. Luke makes no reference to the small size of the mustard seed or the tall plant which it produces, because people were familiar with the proverb (Lk 13:19). The Jewish rabbis spoke of the breaches of the law "as small as a mustard seed." Jesus spoke of having faith the size of a mustard seed which, as he said, would be quite sufficient for doing the impossible (Mt 17:20).

The small mustard seed produced a rather tall shrub. It is estimated that it grew to a height of 8 to 12 feet. Because it grows to such a height, it is called a "tree." It may be that Jesus used the word "tree" because that was an Old Testament symbol for a powerful kingdom, which protects its dependent states. In Ezekiel 17:23 we read, "on the mountain heights of Israel I will plant it; it will produce branches and bear fruit and become a splendid cedar. Birds of every kind will nest in it; they will find shelter in the shade of its branches." We find similar language in Daniel 4:20-22. In his interpretation of Nebuchadnezzar's dream, Daniel explains that the tree he saw with its top reaching heaven and filling the earth was his kingdom, and in it the "birds of the air had nests." Both the shade and the seeds of the mustard tree attracted birds, and often they built their nests in its branches. The verb ***kataskenoo*** means to settle, take up quarters, roost.

The parable is very short, but in spite of its brevity, it underscores the big contrast between the insignificant beginnings of the kingdom of heaven and its glorious future. Nothing is said about the mustard seed itself (other than its size), nothing about its use, its color, its taste. But that is not required to make the point of the parable. It is an example taken from everyday life. In our modem society, where we buy our food at the supermarket, we are not always as familiar with the plant world of the Bible as Jesus' hearers would have been.

B. The Meaning

At first blush the parable seems to teach simply that great things often come from small causes, or from inconspicuous beginnings. But this is a kingdom parable, and so we must not content ourselves with drawing psychological or moral observations from this figure of speech. We have to understand this parable in the context of Jesus' ministry. At the moment the kingdom which Jesus brought and proclaimed seemed rather insignificant. Jesus himself was born and grew up in humble circumstances. He did not even have a place where to lay his head. He surrounded himself with a few uneducated fishermen. Among his disciples were some who had a rather shady past, but who had pledged their loyalty to Jesus. The whole adventure did not seem all that promising. This parable gave his followers the assurance that the kingdom which Jesus established would grow and in the end be a glorious kingdom.

The mustard tree grows up rather rapidly, but Jesus did not intend to emphasize the rapid growth of his kingdom. In fact he doesn't seem to put the emphasis on the process of the growth of the kingdom at all. Rather, Jesus wants to assure his followers that the present kingdom is like a tiny mustard seed, but in God's time it will become great. The disciples of Jesus evidently expected the kingdom, God's reign, to take on huge dimensions in their life time. James and John even asked for the privilege of sitting at the right and left of Christ in his glory (Mk 10:3 5). Even after the resurrection the apostles still wonder when the kingdom will emerge (Acts 1:6). Jesus in effect is telling them, that it won't be until the end of the age that the kingdom will appear in all its glory.

Whether the birds, mentioned in the parable, have any theological significance, has been widely debated. Some scholars say, that they are mentioned by Jesus because in some instances in the Old Testament they represent Gentile nations. From this it could be inferred that the kingdom will take on huge dimensions because of the many Gentiles who will respond to the gospel and enter the kingdom. Evidently some rabbis called Gentiles "birds of the air." Whether the birds in this parable are significant or not, we know from other sayings of Jesus, that the gospel of the kingdom is to be proclaimed to all nations before the end will come (Mt 24:14).

It must have been encouraging for his disciples, who in the days of Jesus saw little evidence of the vast contours that God's reign would take on, to be assured that the end would be glorious. Also, it cautioned them against expecting the culmination of the kingdom which Jesus brought, to be manifested in their lifetime. He taught them to pray, "Your kingdom come!" This kingdom was already present in the person and ministry of Jesus, but it would reach its climax when the present age came to an end and the heavenly kingdom dawned in all its glory.

For us today it is important to learn from this parable not to become discouraged when the work of the kingdom runs into obstacles and is resisted and opposed. We are on the winning side. God's kingdom is invincible. We must not interpret the growth of God's kingdom during this interim between Pentecost and *Parousia* in terms of the number of religious organizations, Christian institutions, or even the rejection or acceptance of biblical principles by our secular society. In spite of opposition, and even persecution, God's kingdom will never fail. The apostle John heard a voice from heaven, after his vision of the defeat of the dragon by Michael and his angels, which said:

"Now have come the salvation and power and the kingdom of our God and the authority of his Messiah" (Rev 12:10). With that assurance we can live and labor and wait and, should it be in God's plan, even suffer for the cause of God's kingdom.

II. THE LEAVEN

A. The Parable

"He told them another parable: 'The kingdom of heaven is like yeast that a woman took and mixed in with three measures of flour until all of it was leavened'" (Mt 13:33).

The parable of the mustard seed has a farmer or gardener at the centre of the action; in this parable we get a picture of a woman, a housewife, who is baking bread. Most of the baking in Jesus' day was done in households. Yeast, traditionally called "leaven" in our English Bibles, was required to make the bread rise. Leaven was leftover from previous baking. Sour dough, stored away and then subjected to fermenting juices was used as yeast.

Although they are not mentioned, there were other ingredients that went into the process of baking bread. But we should remember, that this is a parable of the kingdom of heaven and not a recipe for making bread.

The housewife would mix the flour with water, yeast, and a pinch of salt, and then wait until the dough was fermented. That the woman "hides" the yeast in the flour may be strange language, but the meaning is clear; she mixes it with the flour and it then becomes part of the dough. It can no longer be seen, but it causes the entire lump of dough to rise. The proverb, "A little leaven leavens the whole lump," arose from the pervasive character of the yeast. Some scholars suggest that there is here at least an oblique reference to the hiddenness of the kingdom of God in the ministry of Jesus. Repeatedly, for example, Jesus told people whom he had healed, not to tell anyone. Jesus is fully conscious of being Messiah, but he doesn't proclaim his messiahship; he prefers to call himself "Son of Man."

What has often puzzled Bible readers is that a housewife would mix the yeast with "three measures of flour." That's about fifty pounds (one measure was about 13 litres). One could feed a large household with that amount of bread. Perhaps we should be thinking of a festive occasion. The German New Testament scholar, Joachim Jeremias, suggests that the divine visit which Abraham received (Gen 18:6), is in the background here. There Abraham instructs Sarah to knead "three measures of fine meal" and bake cakes for the heavenly visitors. A "three-measure" baking evidently became symbolic for an offering suitable for a heavenly visitor. Also, when Hannah dedicated Samuel at the house of the Lord in Shiloh, she offered among other things an *epha* (i.e., three measures) of flour (1 Sam 1:24). And the same amount is mentioned in the case of Gideon who was visited by an angel (Jdg 6:19). However, the three measures in our parable may also be simply another example of hyperbolic speech, designed to drive home the truth, that only a little bit of yeast is needed for a big batch of dough. And with that we turn to the interpretation of this parable.

B. The Meaning

There may have been something shocking about this parable, for in the thinking of Jewish listeners, leaven (yeast) was associated with evil. The feast of unleavened bread just before Passover (sometimes identified with Passover) engraved that feeling. Prior to the festival the entire house had to be carefully cleaned of all leaven in preparation for this solemn assembly, when the Exodus from Egypt was celebrated (Ex 12:17-20). At the time of the Exodus the people were in such a hurry, that they did not have time to let the bread rise, and so they ate unleavened bread. And that became the standard practice at the annual commemoration of Israel's escape from Egypt. Also, it was forbidden to use leaven in any of the sacrifices (Ex 23:18; 34:24). And so leaven came to symbolize uncleanness, evil.

That this was so can be seen clearly from New Testament references in which leaven symbolizes evil. For example, in 1 Corinthians 5:6-8 Paul quotes the proverb, "A little yeast leavens the whole batch of dough." And he follows that up with the exhortation to "clean out the old yeast so that you may be a new batch, as you really are unleavened." He wants the Corinthians to be daily celebrants of Passover, but "not with old yeast, the yeast of malice and evil, but with unleavened bread of sincerity and truth." We might also recall the warning of Jesus to keep away from "the leaven of the Pharisees and Sadducees" (Mt 10:6)—perhaps a reference to the hostility of both of these sects to the message of Jesus. In any case leaven symbolizes evil.

However, it does not always symbolize evil, and it would be perverse to understand leaven in our parable as representing something evil, when in fact Jesus uses it as an illustration for the growth of the kingdom of God. In some Dispensationalist circles leaven is understood to portray false doctrine which pervades apostate churches. But Jesus nowhere speaks of an apostate church. In our parable leaven represents something good. A figure of speech can be used in more than one way. We all know that Satan is portrayed as a lion (1 Pet 5:8), but so is Christ; he is the Lion of the tribe of Judah.

In our parable we again see the huge contrast between the small beginnings of the kingdom of God in the person and ministry of Jesus and the great results. Although some Bible readers prefer to put the emphasis on the gradual growth of the kingdom, others suggest that, as in the case of the parable of the mustard seed, the emphasis lies on the final victory of the kingdom of heaven. At the moment, when Jesus told these parables to his Jewish audiences, the work which he was beginning seemed so insignificant, but he assured his followers that the kingdom which he was inaugurating would some day surpass all the kingdoms of this earth. Christ's kingdom is invincible (Heb 12:28). Small though it may have appeared in the days of Jesus, there was to be expansion, growth. The yeast would keep on exercising its transforming power. Although the main emphasis may not lie on the process of the growth of the kingdom, it would not be wrong to speak of the transforming power of the message of the kingdom. It transforms individuals, families, communities; it lifts up womanhood, overcomes child exposure and abuse; it makes an end of slavery, and many other evils that tend to plague human societies. The main emphasis, however, lies on the end-result of the leavening process, when the eternal kingdom in all its glory will appear.

Just as one should avoid interpretations that suggest that leaven always stands for evil in the kingdom of God, so one should also avoid other attempts at allegory. For example, some take the woman to represent the church; the three measures of flour for three branches of the human race (Jews, Greeks, Samaritans). But such attempts are completely arbitrary and rob the parable of its basic thrust. Rather, like the parable of the mustard seed, it contrasts the insignificance of the beginnings of the kingdom with its grand finale.

For those of us who are praying for God's kingdom to come and who are working to extend the reign of God, these two parables are a great encouragement. Sometimes we may feel that our contribution to the growth of the kingdom is so paltry, but in the words of the prophet, we should not despise the day of little things (Zech 4:10). The kingdom of heaven was inaugurated with the birth of a baby; it was established with the shameful death of Messiah on a cross. But by his resurrection, Christ broke the power of sin and death, and by the gift of the Spirit of the risen Christ at Pentecost, God has begun his powerful reign over the hearts and lives of those who acknowledge him as King. In spite of temporary set-backs and many failures on the part of the church, as well as the fierce attacks by the evil one, it is only a matter of time and God's kingdom will be manifested in all its glory.

In a fanciful conversation, John Masefield imagines the wife of Pilate, asking the centurion who stood at the cross and saw Christ die, "Do you think he is dead?" "No lady, I don't." "Then where is he?" "Let loose in the world, lady, where neither Roman nor Jew can stop his truth." And to that we can say a hearty "Amen."

CHAPTER ELEVEN

THE TEN MAIDENS Matthew 25:1-13

This woodcut is by an anonymous artist from Christoph Wiegel's **Biblia Ectypa: Bildnesse auss Heiliger Schrift, Alt und Neuen Testament** published in 1695.

THE TEN MAIDENS Matthew 25:1-13

This parable has traditionally been entitled, "The Parable of the Ten Virgins." We can assume that they were virgins, but the parable has nothing to do with virginity. The Greek word *pathenos*, like the Gernan *Jungfrau*, has a double meaning: it can mean virgin, but it can also simply designate a young woman of marriageable age. And the latter is the meaning in our parable. Some modern translators (e.g., the TEV) call it "The Parable of the Ten Girls," but that sounds a bit too colloquial. The NRSV calls it "The Parable of the Ten Bridesmaids," but the problem with that is, that these bridesmaids have little in common with what we call bridesmaids in our culture. Perhaps "The Parable of the Ten Maidens" is a reasonably good choice, although it does sound a bit formal.

Let me begin the interpretation of this parable by putting this story into its wider context. The adverb "then" connects this parable with what was said at the end of Matthew 24. Jesus has just explained that no one knows when the last hour of this present age will strike, not even the angels know that, but only the Father. And because no one knows the time, it is incumbent upon the followers of Jesus to be prepared at all times.

Jesus mentions the days of Noah, when people failed to listen to Noah's warnings and consequently were overwhelmed when the Flood came. "That's how it will be when the Son of Man comes" (Mt 24:39). Other illustrations are found in verses 40 and 41: two men will be working in a field; one will be taken away, the other left behind. Two women will be grinding meal together; one will be taken away, the other left behind. And these illustrations are followed up with the exhortation: "Watch out, then, because you do not know what day your Lord will come" (v. 42). Another illustration is that of a householder. If he knew when a thief planned to break in, he would stay awake and guard his house. And then follows the exhortation: "So then, you also must be ready, because the Son of Man will come at an hour when you are not expecting him" (v. 44). Finally, Jesus gives us a short parable of a landlord who intends to be away for some time and who puts a steward in charge of his servants. A good steward has no fear of the sudden return of his master, because he has been faithful during his absence. The unfaithful servant, on the other hand, will be punished severely.

All these illustrations focus on the end of this age, when Christ returns. They are eschatological parables, and they form the background to the parable of the ten maidens, which ends with the exhortation to be watchful, always ready to meet the Lord. Let us then expand on this story and put it into its first-century cultural setting! We will then follow this up with an application to our own lives.

I. THE PARABLE (25:1-12)

"Then the kingdom of the heavens will be like this."

A young girl who knew her Bible stories was asked on one occasion which parts of the Bible she liked best. Her answer was, "the like stories." She meant, of course, the parables, in which we hear the phrase over and over again, "the kingdom of God is like." All the parables of Jesus are "kingdom" parables, even when the word itself is not mentioned in the text. And where Matthew prefers to speak of "the kingdom of the heavens," Mark and Luke have "the kingdom of God." Clearly there is no difference in meaning; rather it is a cultural preference. Matthew has Jewish readers in mind, and they tended to use the name "God" sparingly, using surrogates instead. One of these substitutes for "God" was "heaven." When the prodigal son repented of his waywardness, he confessed, "Father, I have sinned against heaven [God] and you" (Lk 15:2 1). Since the word heaven in Hebrew is always in the plural, it is plural also in the Greek of our passage.

So then, what is the kingdom of the heavens like? It

is likened to ten maidens who took their lamps and went out to meet the bridegroom (25:1). Although we do not know all the details of Jewish wedding customs in the first century, we have sufficient information to be able to put all this into its cultural context. Dr. J. A. Findlay, in *Jesus and His Parables*, tells of nearing a Galilean town in his car some fifty years ago, when he saw a group of young ladies all dressed up, playing musical instruments and dancing along the road. His guide then explained that they were going to keep the bride company until the bridegroom arrived. Findlay then wondered whether he might attend the wedding, but was told that that was hardly possible, since the wedding could take place either tonight or even tomorrow. The bridegroom might come unexpectedly even in the middle of the night, and so the bridal party had to be ready at any time to go out to meet him. And once the bridegroom arrived, and the guests had entered the reception room, the door would be shut and latecomers would not be admitted.

Findlay's experience in the 20th century illustrates some of the wedding customs reflected in our parable. Obviously some traditions do not die easily. In our story we see ten maidens, friends of the bride, who went out to meet the bridegroom. They were going to wait until he arrived with his friends to conduct the bride to his house for the wedding. Christians should be aware of the fact, that church weddings are a much later innovation; in Israel, weddings were family celebrations. All ten maidens go out to meet the bridegroom. (There are a few manuscripts which have "to meet the bridegroom and the bride," but "and the bride" is a later addition by some copyist, for he noticed that otherwise the bride is nowhere mentioned. But that is not the correct reading and, in fact, would distort the picture, for they were with the bride, waiting for the bridegroom to come.) What these young ladies did was, they went to the house of the bride and kept her company. Then when the messenger would come and announce that the bridegroom was on his way, they would all go out to meet him, and together with the bride they would go to the bridegroom's house, where the marriage would take place.

Since it was night, the ten maidens all took "lamps" with them. These may have been the common oil lamps found in every home in those days. But the Greek word *lampros* can also mean "torches," as it does in John 18:3, where the soldiers come with lanterns and torches to capture Jesus.

Torches were simply sticks with rags wrapped around one end and dipped in oil. The oil would burn for about 15 minutes and then fresh oil would have to be added. For outside use, torches were preferable to oil lamps, which the wind could easily blow out.

Five of these maidens were foolish and five were wise (v. 2). The foolish ones took their lamps but did not take any extra oil with them, whereas the wise took containers full of oil for their lamps. Evidently they all oiled their torches to begin with (if, in fact, they were torches), but only five of them had extra oil to replenish their lamps. (I remember when I was a boy, I listened to our fathers at a Bible study, arguing over what the oil or was it the oil cans represented. But that kind of allegory is foreign to our text. The lamps and the oil are simply part of the scenery, the staging.)

As the bridegroom was delayed, they all got drowsy and fell asleep (v. 5). In our society it would be an unforgivable faux pas for a bridegroom to let the wedding party wait on tenterhooks so long, but in Jesus' day things were done differently. Sometimes the bridegroom was delayed because the two families hadn't yet agreed on the details of the marriage settlement. A long process of haggling over the bride price might be seen as a sign that she was worth very much. Sometimes the wedding was delayed because the groom had not yet paid the bride price. When we taught in Nairobi, an African colleague proudly told us how many cows he had paid for his wife, and that he still owed his father-in-law several cows. Jesus is telling a "likely story," that was well understood by his hearers, and so there is no need for him to explain to his hearers what the cause of the delay might have been in this case.

This parable was significant in the later church, when the question of the "delay" of Christ's second coming was often raised. And it is still a relevant question, because the church, after two thousand years, is still waiting for the Bridegroom to come. I think we would all agree that the bridegroom in our parable represents Christ. That was a bold move on the part of Jesus, for in the Old Testament, God is Israel's Bridegroom and Israel is his bride. But this is not the only instance in which what was said of God in the Old Testament is transferred to Jesus in the New.

Perhaps it should be mentioned also, the word "delay," when applied to Christ's return, should not be understood in a negative sense, as if God's schedule somehow was interrupted and that he fell behind. There were scoffers already in the first century who doubted Christ's promise to come again (2 Peter 3). The apostle Peter answers them by pointing out that God has a different view of time than we have; with him a thousand years are like a day. Also, he mentions those who mocked Noah who prepared an ark on dry land, but were wiped out by the flood when it came eventually. Moreover, what seems like a delay, is really an extension of this age of grace, for God is waiting for all people to repent and turn to him in faith.

Because the bridegroom delayed, all ten of our maidens got weary with waiting and all of them dozed off. Perhaps by the time the two families had worked out the details of the marriage covenant it was midnight. The young ladies were fast asleep when they heard the shout, "Here's the bridegroom. Come for a meeting with him" (v. 6). The word for "meeting" (*apantesis*) is the same as that in 1 Thessalonians 4:17, where Christ comes with the shout of the archangel, to gather his church for a "meeting" with the Lord in the air. It's a formal word for a reception. In Acts 28:15 we read of Roman Christians who went out to Three Taverns for a meeting with Paul as he arrived as prisoner; they went out to "receive" him.

When the word came that the bridegroom was approaching, the ten girls woke up (v. 7) and trimmed their lamps. They are not criticized for their slumber, both wise and foolish fell asleep. That is true to life. Waking and sleeping is something that believers who are waiting for the Lord's return do as well. The difference between the wise and the foolish was that the wise had taken extra oil with them; they were prepared for a delay. To infer from the parable that half the church will be asleep when Jesus returns and will miss the marriage supper of the Lamb, would not be sound hermeneutics.

With the news that the bridegroom was on his way, the young ladies are all awake, and they trim their lamps. The word "trimmed" is used here a bit loosely. If oil lamps are meant, it would mean that they poured oil into their clay lamps and adjusted the wicks; if torches, they poured fresh oil on them or they re-lit them. It was then that the five foolish maidens discovered their negligence. And they say to the wise, "Let us have some of your oil, because our lamps are going out" (v. 8). The verb for "going out" is in the present tense, suggesting linear action. In our imagination we can see the flames flickering and finally going out.

The foolish maidens want the wise to share their extra oil with them, but the request is declined. Better to have five torches all the way to the bridegroom's house, then ten only part of the way. And so they are advised to go to the dealers and buy some for themselves. We should not infer from the turn of events, that the parable encourages selfishness; that would be contrary to everything that Jesus taught. There may be a suggestion here that no one can depend on the preparedness of the next person, but that may be overly subtle. This parable is not a lesson on the Golden Rule, and the wise maidens are not criticized for not sharing their oil with those who asked for it.

So the five foolish girls leave to find oil. On the occasion of a small village wedding most people would still be awake at midnight, and it would have been possible to obtain some oil. Or, they may have gone to a merchant who sold olive oil, woke him up and bought some. But it was too late. "While they went to buy it, the bridegroom came, and those who were ready went with him into the wedding banquet; and the door was shut" (v. 10). The five girls with flaming torches to light their way, would have escorted the bride and the bridegroom to the groom's house, where the marriage celebration would take place. That shutting of the door makes the point, that in God's dealing with humans, there is such a thing as "too late." The writer to the Hebrews repeats over and over again (chaps. 3-4), "The Holy Spirit says, Today when you hear his voice, do not harden your hearts."

Later the other maidens come also, saying "Lord, lord open up to us" (v. 11), but he replied, "Truly I tell you, I do not know you" (v. 12).

The word "lord" is here the polite word of address and is best understood as an equivalent to the English "sir," the German "***Herr***," the French "***monsieur***." Jesus may, however, have intended the word to be an allusion to Christ, the Lord, who some day will be the Judge of all humankind, and even if the word "lord" here refers only to the bridegroom in the story, we can assume that the bridegroom represents Christ. It is Christ who in the end will decide who will attend the messianic marriage supper and who will be excluded.

The maidens who came too late must have called repeatedly for the bridegroom himself to come to the door, but it was too late. His answer to their petition is:

"Amen, Amen, I say to you, I do not know you." That reminds us of Matthew 7:23, where at the end of the Sermon on the Mount, Jesus says, that on the last day some people will say, "Lord, lord...did we not prophecy in your name and cast out demons, and do many deeds of power in your name?" Then he will declare to them, "I never knew you, go away from me, you evildoers." In Rabbinic literature, "I do not know you," was an idiomatic way of saying, "I don't want anything to do with you." For example, when Peter denied his Lord, he said, "I do not know the man" (Mt 26:72). For a teacher to say to a student, "I do not know you," meant that he was expelled.

Our parable ends with a closed door. The foolish maidens had missed the opportunity to participate in the wedding festivities and the marriage banquet. Jesus rounds the story off with an exhortation: "Keep awake therefore, for you know neither the day nor the hour" (v. 13). And with that we have come to the application of this parable to our lives.

II. THE APPLICATION

When Jesus told this parable he was addressing a Jewish audience, his fellow countrymen. By his teaching he was inviting those who repented to become members of the kingdom of God. Christ was the Bridegroom who was inviting his contemporaries to the messianic banquet, we might say. The original hearers must also have heard the note of warning in this parable, not to be indifferent to the opportunity God was offering them, for the time would come when it would be too late to make that decision.

But when Matthew wrote his Gospel, there was already a Christian church, spreading all over the Roman empire. For them the message of the parable was: be prepared for the return of the Bridegroom, Christ's second coming. And that is also the basic message for us in the 21st century. Before we say more about watchfulness as we continue to wait for the Lord's return, let me mention a few items that the parable does not teach. First, we should not infer from the parable that Christ's coming will be at night. Some early Christians held that view, but they didn't yet know that the earth was round, and when it was night in the Near East it was day on the other side of the globe. As a child, for some reason or another, I felt that Christ would come at night. One night I dreamt that in fact he had come, and I was very frightened, for I did not want to be left behind. So I got up and went into my parents' bedroom to see if they were still there, and since they were sincere Christians, I went back to bed, thankful that Christ had not yet come, for I didn't think I was ready.

Also, we should not try to read meanings into the details of this parable story. Some have identified the oil that the maidens needed for their lamps as representing our good works. But, can one buy good works? Such applications are arbitrary, for there are others who have suggested that the oil represents the Holy Spirit. Moreover, we should not infer from this parable that the church will be in a sad spiritual state when Christ returns, and that only half of those who claim the name of Christ will enter the eternal kingdom. The foolish maidens do not represent a specific group within the church; neither do the wise, for that matter.

The parable emphasizes once again (as in Mt 24) that we should not try to speculate about the time of Christ's coming, for Jesus says clearly that we do not know the day or the hour (Mt 24:13). (Some have argued, since he didn't say the month or the year, it is quite legitimate for Bible readers to try to establish a date for the Parousia; but that is a violation of Jesus' words.) The parable is a call to all Christian believers to be ready when Christ returns. What the parable does not do, is to give us instructions on what it means to be prepared at all times for the Lord's return. But parables are not designed to teach all aspects of the Christian life; for that we must turn to other passages of the Scriptures. The basic message of the parable is: keep spiritually awake!

And how does one do this? By constantly thinking or speaking of Christ's return? Hardly! It means rather to keep the lamp of faith, hope and love burning. By prayer, repentance, striving for holiness, without which no one will see the Lord, we will keep spiritually alert. To wait for the Lord's return means to fulfill our calling here on earth, to contribute to the ongoing work of Christ's kingdom; it means to be good stewards of the gifts of God. Readiness does not mean to live nervously, constantly looking for signs of the coming end. It means to go about our daily tasks as children of the day, who have the assurance from God's word, that they will not be caught off guard when that great day comes.

Perhaps a practical illustration might help us to understand preparedness for Christ's coming. A housewife expects guests for dinner. She waits for them. How? by sitting down nervously in an easy chair and biting her fingernails? Hardly! She may be quite relaxed, as she cleans the house, peels the potatoes, sets the table. Perhaps she sings a song or hums a tune as she goes about her household duties. She may not even be thinking constantly of the coming of the guests; she focuses on what needs to be done in order to be ready when they arrive. And so we wait for Christ's return by being faithful in our generation in the tasks that God has assigned to us. Since we do not know how soon he will come, we have to take into account another possibility, namely our own death. As we look into the future we see two horizons: on the one hand, we know that if Christ tarries much longer, we will die and go to be with the Lord; on the other hand, when we go to bed in the evening we might say to ourselves, before the morning dawns we may be caught up to meet the Lord in the clouds, as Paul puts it. May God help us to be ready at all times!

CHAPTER TWELVE

THE SHEEP AND THE GOATS
Matthew 25:31-46

This woodcut is by an anonymous artist from Christoph Wiegel's **Biblia Ectypa: Bildnesse auss Heiliger Schrift, Alt und Neuen Testament** published in 1695.

THE SHEEP AND THE GOATS Matthew 25:31-46

Jesus began his ministry by announcing that the kingdom of God had come near (Mk 1:15). This kingdom had no geographical borders and it was not political in nature. It was the reign of God over the hearts and lives of people that Jesus had come to establish. A great many of Jesus' countrymen repented, believed the good news, and thereby became members of God's kingdom. After the outpouring of the Spirit at Pentecost, this new community, that emerged in the days of Jesus, was known as the church of Jesus Christ. Today God's sovereign reign is acknowledged by millions of people all over the world. The kingdom of God (or heaven) has by now been a present reality for almost 2000 years. But we still pray, "May your kingdom come." That means that there is a future dimension to God's kingdom which has not yet been realized. The kingdom which Jesus established still awaits a glorious climax at the end of the age.

A number of Jesus' parable focus on that climax. We call them eschatological parables. The parable of the sheep and the goats is one of them. The word "eschatological" is derived from two Greek words: *eschatos*, meaning "last," and *logos*, meaning "word." It means, then, the word or the teaching about the last things. Like the parable of the ten maidens, the parable we are about to study, focuses on the final judgment which takes place when Christ returns. The apostle Paul puts it this way: "We must all appear before the judgment seat of Christ, so that each may receive recompense for what has been done in the body, whether good or evil" (2 Cor 5:10). Let us then go through this parable verse by verse.

I. THE JUDGE: THE SON OF MAN (v.31 a)

"When the Son of Man comes in the glory and all the angels with him, then he will sit on the throne of glory."

References to the future coming of the Son of Man appear here and there in all the Gospels. In Matthew 16:27, for example, we read, "For the Son of Man is to come with his angels in the glory of his Father, and then he will repay everyone for what has been done." In Matthew 24:30,31 we have something similar: "Then the sign of the Son of Man will appear in heaven, and then all the tribes of the earth will mourn, and they will see the Son of Man coming in clouds of heaven with power and great glory. And he will send out his angels with a loud trumpet call, and they will gather his elect from the four winds, from one end of heaven to the other."

"Son of Man" is the most common self-designation of Jesus. This title occurs 81 times in the Gospels. Outside the Gospels it occurs only once, namely in Acts 7:56, where Stephen, as he was stoned to death, saw the Son of Man standing to welcome him home and to defend him, when he was falsely accused and shamefully put to death. It was a Christological title which the church did not, for some reason or other, perpetuate. Perhaps Christians felt that it was not sufficiently clear in its meaning and didn't say quite what Christ, who was seated at the right hand of God, meant to them. It is not found in any of the 21 letters of the New Testament.

The Son of Man sayings fall into three categories in the Gospels. Sometimes "Son of Man" is simply a Semitic equivalent for "I." When Jesus said, "The Son of Man is lord of the Sabbath," he meant "I am the lord of the Sabbath." Then there are other Son of Man sayings that are connected with Christ's suffering and death. For example, "The Son of Man has come not to be served but to serve and to give his life a ransom for many" (Mk 10:45). But then there is a third group of Son of Man sayings, in which the Son of Man comes in his glory. And that is what we have in our parable. The Son of Man comes, as Jesus said in Matthew 13:26, "in clouds with great power and glory." But let me add a few more comments on the "Son of Man" title!

The question is often asked, why didn't Jesus simply speak of himself as Messiah, rather than Son of Man? He never denied that he was Messiah. He was fully conscious of the fact that he was Messiah. But Messiahship was misunderstood rather badly in Jesus' day. Had he called himself Messiah, people would have thought of him as a political or military leader who intended to overthrow the Roman power and restore Israel to its former greatness. But Jesus made it very plain that his kingdom was not of this world.

The title "Son of Man" very likely has its background in Daniel 7:13 where we have a picture of one like the Son of Man coming in clouds of heaven, to whom an eternal kingdom is given. Jesus found this title useful, for it had undertones of humanity, but it also had overtones of deity. The Son of Man came to die, but he will come again in glory at the end of the age. In our parable we see the Son of Man in his exalted, glorious state.

II. CHRIST' S COMING IN GLORY (v.31 b)

The Son of Man, said Jesus, "will come in his glory." This is a reference to Christ's second coming. The return of Christ at the end of the age is called his ***parousia***. The word means presence, coming, arrival in its everyday usage. For example, Paul rejoices at the ***parousia*** of Stephanas (1 Cor 16:17). However, the word also had a technical meaning. It was used to describe the arrival of the emperor for an official visit, and was always celebrated with great pomp and circumstance. We have a papyrus scrap from those days which reads, "Let us labor night and day [to get the town into shape], for the ***parousia*** of the emperor is near." This secular word was picked up by the writers of the New Testament and applied to the glorious arrival of Christ at the end of the age.

Christ's coming is also called his "revelation" (***apokalupsis***). The Corinthians are said to be waiting "for the revelation of our Lord Jesus Christ (1 Cor 1:7). To the Thessalonians Paul writes that Jesus "will be revealed from heaven with his mighty angels" (2 Thess 1:7). A third significant word used to designate Christ's coming is that of his "appearance" (***epiphaneia***).

Timothy is challenged to do his work in the light of "the appearing of our Lord Jesus Christ" (1 Tim 6:14). Paul is certain that Christ will reward him and "all who have loved his appearing" (2 Tim 4:8).

In our parable, however, we have the simple verb "coming." This verb (***erchomai***) is often found in eschatological contexts. Jesus said that he would come as a thief in the night (Mt 24:42). The New Testament closes with this assurance: "Surely, I am coming soon" (Rev 22:20). And the writer to the Hebrews even speaks of Christ coming "a second time" (9:28). And when he comes, he will come in "glory." That is in vivid contrast to his first coming, which was so lowly, that people found it hard to believe that he was God's Son, the Messiah.

The Greek word for "glory" (***doxa***) had no religious connotations in secular society, but when the Old Testament was translated into Greek (beginning in the 3rd century B.C.), ***doxa*** became the translation of the Hebrew word ***kabod***, and that changed ***doxa*** into a profoundly religious word. It now referred to God's manifested presence and power, his majesty and splendor. Professor Caird of Oxford says of the translators of the Hebrew Old Testament into Greek, that they decided to pay the Greek word extra, and make it work overtime. In our passage ***doxa*** refers to the power and majesty of Christ's return. Christ's coming in glory is pictured in a variety of ways in the New Testament, and we must not focus on one picture to the exclusion of others.

When the Son of Man comes in his glory all the angels will be with him. That's an echo of Zechariah 14:5, "Then the Lord my God will come and all the holy angels with him." Angels attend all the great events of salvation history; they were there at Christ's birth; they came to him after his temptations by the devil; they were present at the empty tomb; they spoke to the apostles when Christ ascended into glory. It is only natural, then, that these denizens of heaven should attend Christ's second coming.

And when he comes in glory he will sit upon his glorious throne. That was anticipated already in Matthew 19:28, where Jesus promises his disciples that they too will sit with him on twelve thrones when "the Son of Man is seated on his throne of glory."

III. THE JUDGE UPON THE THRONE (v.31 c)

In the Old Testament, as well as in the New, God is portrayed as the Judge of all the earth, as Abraham called him (Gen 18:25). But Jesus explains in John 5:27, that the Father has given the Son "authority to execute judgment because he is the Son of Man." In Paul's Areopagus address the apostle says, that God has fixed a day on which he will judge the world in righteousness by a man whom he has appointed, and of this he has given assurance to all, by raising him from the dead" (Acts 17:31). Clearly the one whom he raised from the dead is the one by whom the world will be judged. And so we must not try to drive a wedge between God and Christ, when it comes to carrying out the last judgment.

The Son of Man will sit on his glorious throne. The throne of God was a very important concept in Judaism. It was thought to be one of the seven things that existed even before the world was created, and that was their way of saying that it is extremely important. Perhaps nowhere in the New Testament is the concept of "throne" so important as in the last book of the Bible, where God is constantly referred to as "the Sitting One" (*ho kathemenos*) When I was still a seminary student and had to write a final exam on the book of Revelation, we were asked, among other things, to trace the concept of "throne" through the book. The book ends with a vision of God sitting on "the great white throne" (Rev 20), condemning those whose names were not found in the book of life. But in Revelation 22 we see the other side of the coin; here a river of water of life proceeds from the throne of God and the Lamb. And all who belong to Christ will reign with him forever and ever.

The topic of final judgment is not a palatable subject in our day. It's the last thing modern man wants to hear about. The notion that human beings are accountable to a holy and righteous God for what they have done in this life (or failed to do), does not sit well with people generally. However, if we want to be faithful to the scriptures, we cannot avoid this topic. Some years ago Newsweek did a survey and found that 77% of all Americans believed in heaven, but when it came to the question of judgment, the percentage dropped considerably. But the writer to the Hebrews says that "judgment" belongs to the elementary Christian doctrines, to the ABC's of the gospel (6:1,2). If there were no final judgment, we would have to ask, why God would seek the salvation of humanity through the sacrifice of his only Son, Jesus Christ, who delivers us from the coming wrath (1 Thess 1:10). Scholars have observed that 12 of 36 longer parables of Jesus have the theme of judgment in them. Also, the word "hell" (*geena* in Greek) is found almost exclusively in the mouth of Jesus, the kindest person that ever lived. Even in John 3:16, which is the gospel in a nutshell, we read that God gave his only Son, so that people should not perish.

IV. THE FINAL SEPARATION OF HUMANITY (vv. 32,33)

"And all the nations will be gathered before him, and he will separate people one from another as a shepherd separates the sheep from the goats. And he will put the sheep to the right hand and the goats to the left."

The passive voice of the verb "gathered," suggests that God will do the gathering (this is sometimes called the divine passive). On the other hand, in the parable of the wheat and the weeds (Mt 13), we are told, that the harvest is the end of the world and that the reapers are the angels. In Revelation 14:14,15, the apostle John has a vision of one who looks like the Son of Man with a golden crown on his head. And an angel calls out, "Use your sickle and reap, for the harvest of the earth is ripe." Different images portray the same event.

There has been some dispute over the meaning of "all nations." And that's due in part to the fact that the Greek word ***ethnos*** can mean Gentiles, pagans, heathen, unbelievers, or simply "people." (German translations usually have, "***Voelker***" [people] not nations.) Here are some ways in which the word has been understood by interpreters of this parable:

(a) Some Bible readers have understood the word nations to refer to Gentiles not to Jews. But the line between Jew and Gentile disappears in the New Testament, as far as salvation is concerned. Rather, it is drawn between believers and unbelievers, be they Jew or Gentile. It would be strange if the Jews were exempted from final judgment, and the New Testament suggests no such thing.

(b) Others have suggested that this is a judgment of non-Christians only, whether Jews or Gentiles. But the conclusion of this parable makes it plain that there will be a separation in the end of the genuine followers of Christ and those who are not members of Christ's family.

(c) Still others have argued for the exact opposite, and hold that this is a judgment of Christians. That believers will also appear before the judgment seat of Christ, is stated in 2 Corinthians 5:10. Our works will be evaluated, tested, as 1 Corinthians 3:1-14 describes this. But the outcome of the judgment of believers is not heaven or hell, as we have it in this parable, but whether their works will stand up to God's fire test and whether they will be rewarded or not.

(d) Most scholars agree that this parable focuses on all humanity. The New Jerusalem Bible in a footnote explains the word "nations," because of the ambiguity of the word, in this way: "every human being of every period of history." And the TEV has, "all the people of all nations." The German Good News translation has, "*alle Voelker der Erde*" (all the people of this earth). What we should definitely avoid is, to read our modem concept of nation-states into this word, as if the countries of this world, as we know them now, will be judged as countries.

Jesus compares this division of the peoples of this earth to the separation of sheep and goats. Sheep and goats were often herded together. That was more economical for it required only one shepherd for the entire flock. Also, the restless goats kept the herd moving, so that vegetation was not destroyed completely by their intense grazing habits. When I visited Israel for the first time some 35 years ago, I saw first hand, how sheep and goats were herded together, even in modern times. However, when evening comes, the two are separated by the shepherd. Goats need a warmer place than sheep. The shepherd stands at the gate with his shepherd's crook and taps the individual sheep and goat on the nose to guide them into their respective stalls for the night. This is the cultural setting of this parable. What is said here of the separation of sheep and goats, is said also of the separation of the good and bad fish in the parable of the fishnet (Mt 13:49).

Why the sheep represent the righteous and the goats the wicked in our parable is not explained. Both were valued for their meat, their hide and their milk. Some think sheep were more valuable. Perhaps it was because already the Old Testament pictures Israel as God's flock of sheep, not goats. "We are the sheep of his pasture," says the Psalmist.

When the last day comes the divine Shepherd will place the sheep on his right hand, but the goats to the left. Sheep and goats of course represent people; the sheep are the righteous and the goats are the ungodly. Right and left in Israel, as in many cultures, often symbolized favor and disfavor, fortune and misfortune, honor and dishonor (no offence here to those who are left-handed). The Latin word for "left" is ***sinister***, which has a pejorative meaning in English, and the word "right" (***dexter***) has a positive meaning (skilful, adroit).

V. THE BLESSED OF THE FATHER (v. 34)

"Then the king will say to those at his right hand, 'Come O blessed of my father, inherit the kingdom prepared for you from the foundation of the world'."

The righteous are said to be people who are "being blessed by God, the Father." The verb "bless" (eulogeo in Greek) can have more than one meaning depending on the context. One meaning is, to enjoy the many benefits given graciously by God the Father to his redeemed people. Here they are given the privilege of entering the eternal kingdom. There is another word for "blessed" in the New Testament (***makarios***) which is found, for example, in the Sermon on the Mount. "Blessed are the pure in heart." But that word means "happy," although the English word happy is much too flat a word to describe the blessedness Jesus is talking about in the Beatitudes.

Those on the right hand inherit the kingdom of the Father. The kingdom of the Father is the kingdom of God, the kingdom of the heavens. And since this kingdom is seen here in its future manifestation, to inherit the kingdom is to enter, to possess it. In Matthew 19:29 Jesus said that those who leave everything to follow him, will inherit eternal life, i.e., possess it. The apostle Peter speaks of an inheritance that is imperishable, undefiled, and unfading, kept in heaven for us (1 Pet 1:4).

Although God's kingdom is a present reality today, and we are members of the kingdom by God's grace, there is still a future dimension to this kingdom, which Paul calls "the heavenly kingdom" (2 Tim 4:18). At the last supper Jesus promised, that he would not drink of the fruit of the vine until he drank it anew with them in his Father's kingdom. When Jesus speaks of the kingdom of "my" Father, he indicates that he stands in a different relationship to God then we do. After his resurrection he spoke to Mary Magdalene of "my" Father and "your" Father. His relationship to God is that of essence (of being, ontological), our relationship to God as Father is that of adoption, of new birth, of faith.

The kingdom which the righteous are called upon to possess, was prepared before the foundation of the world. That God is the creator of this universe, is affirmed throughout Scripture. What is interesting here in our text is that God's plan to save people and to bring them into his heavenly kingdom was ready before the creation of the world. We have other passages in the New Testament that witness to this. For example, in Revelation 13:8 the apostle John speaks of the ungodly whose names have not been written in the book of life, of the Lamb, slaughtered from (or before) the foundation of the earth." The Genesis account of creation should, therefore, not be studied independently, but always as the backdrop of God's salvatory plans which he carries out in human history and which he will complete when we reach the heavenly kingdom.

VI. DEEDS OF LOVE AS EVIDENCE OF A GENUINE FAITH (vv.35,36)

We are now given the reason why the righteous are admitted to the eternal kingdom of God and others are shut out. "For I was hungry and you gave me food. I was thirsty and you gave me drink. I was a stranger and you welcomed me. I was naked and you clothed me. I was sick and you visited me. I was in prison and you came to me."

Here we have six situations of need, which illustrate ways in which a living faith expresses itself. They are all deeds of love. Paul writes to the Galatians, "For in Christ Jesus neither circumcision nor uncircumcision counts for anything; the only thing that counts is faith working through love" (Gal 5:6). Bible readers who have grasped the great truth that we are saved by grace and not by works, often get nervous at this point in our parable, for on the surface it appears as if one can gain entrance into the eternal kingdom by helping the needy.

But both Paul and the apostle James clearly teach, that good deeds are but the evidence of a genuine faith. In Ephesians 2:8, where Paul underscores the truth that we are saved by grace through faith and not by works, he adds: "Created in Christ Jesus for good works, which God prepared beforehand to be our way of life" (2:10). And James writes, "What good is it... if you say you have faith, but do not have works? Can faith save you?..Faith by itself; if it has no works, is dead" (2:14).

VII. THEIR RESPONSE TO CHRIST'S COMMENDATION (vv. 37-40)

The righteous are surprised at these words of commendation by the divine Judge. They are delightfully unconscious of all these expressions of love for which they are praised. They didn't keep record of their good deeds; they knew that they couldn't earn their passage to heaven by chalking up a certain number of deeds of mercy. This parable has been called the parable of the great surprises. First, the righteous are surprised; later, it's the ungodly.

While on earth, the godly did not constantly ask themselves, have I done enough good works to merit eternal life? They knew that their salvation was entirely by grace through faith. But their faith manifested itself in deeds of mercy. And these deeds were not forgotten by Christ. "Lord," they ask, "when did we see you hungry and fed you, or thirsty and gave you to drink?" And the King then explains in very authoritative language: "Amen, I say to you, as you did it to one of the least of these my brothers, you did it unto me" (v. 34). What is highly significant in this explanation of Christ, the heavenly Judge, is that the deeds of kindness done to other people, were in fact done to Christ. It is really quite staggering to think, that when we serve other people, we are serving Christ.

Good deeds done to the least of Christ's brothers, of course, includes the sisters. No one questions the inclusive use of "brothers" in our parable. However, there has been considerable debate on who these brothers are:

(a) Since the word "brothers" is often used for "believers" in the New Testament, some interpreters take it to mean fellow Christians. That we should do good to our brothers and sisters in Christ is, of course, clearly taught in the New Testament. "Do good to all people," writes the apostle Paul, "most of all to the household of faith" (Gal 6:10). But there is nothing in this parable, spoken to a Jewish audience prior to Pentecost, to suggest that the deeds of mercy done in Christ's name were done exclusively to fellow believers.

(b) In the system of interpretation, known as Dispensationalism, as developed by the Irishman John Darby in the 19th century, and popularized in America by C. I. Scofield and others, the brothers in our parable are said to be the Jews. And the kingdom of which Jesus speaks here is that of the future millennium. From that it follows, that nations who have been kind to the Jews will enter the millennium, while those who mistreated them will not. But the kingdom which the righteous inherit in this parable is the eternal kingdom and not the millennium; the last verse of the parable makes that clear (v. 45). The ungodly experience eternal punishment and the righteous enter eternal life.

(c) There is another line of interpretation that goes like this: the brothers are Jesus' messengers, his servants. Those who mistreat his servants will suffer dire consequences; those who treat them kindly, have the promise of the kingdom. This view is based in part on Matthew 10:14,15, where Jesus sends out the twelve with these words: "If anyone will not welcome you or listen to your words, shake off the dust from your feet as you leave that house or town. Truly I tell you, it will be more tolerable for the land of Sodom and Gomorrah on the day of judgment than for that town." But our parable doesn't speak to the question of accepting or rejecting God's messengers; it speaks of deeds of love done to those in need.

(d) I would suggest, then, that the best way of reading "brothers" in this parable is "our fellow human beings," whether believers or unbelievers, who are in need. This is the view of the majority of evangelical scholars. The British scholar, Dr. Wenham, writes, "It seems likely, that the traditional view, that Jesus is here identifying with the needy in general is correct." And the American New Testament scholar, Dr. Hagner, of Fuller Theological Seminary, writes: "the reference is to all human beings in need."

VIII. THE JUDGMENT OF THOSE ON THE LEFT (vv. 41-45)

And now we come to the more sombre part of the parable. Those who have no living faith, who have no relationship with Christ, are now in focus. "Then he will say to those at the left hand, 'Depart from me, you cursed, into the eternal fire prepared for the devil and his angels'."

The solemn words "depart from me," are unspeakably sad and remind us of the words of Jesus at the end of the Sermon on the Mount. There Christ says, "I never knew you; go away from me, you evildoers" (Mt 7:23). And Paul writes in 2 Thessalonians 1:9, "These will suffer the punishment of eternal destruction, away from the face of the Lord...when he comes to be glorified by his saints."

There is nothing more tragic than to be separated from God. Moreover, it is stated here, that they are "cursed," meaning that they are under divine judgment, which is here described as "eternal fire." But that was not God's purpose when he created humankind. "Eternal fire," said Jesus, was prepared for the devil and his angels. This is a reference to evil angels who have given their loyalty to Satan. God did not determine in eternity past who would be saved and who would be lost. Hell was not prepared originally for human beings, but for the devil. The ungodly are surprised by this verdict. They expected to do better in the last judgment. But the Judge explains, "Just as you did not do it to one of the least of these, you did not do it to me."

IX. THE ULTIMATE FATE OF HUMANKIND (v. 46)

"And these shall go away into eternal punishment, but the righteous into eternal life." In 1949 a correspondent for the London Daily Telegraph gave this rendering of verse 46: "And these will depart into correction for a period of time, but the just into a period of life." Michael Green, who used to teach at Regent College, vigorously mounted objections to such a distortion of the text. F. F. Bruce, famous Manchester New Testament scholar, points out that the adjective "eternal" stands before the word punishment and so one cannot say that this punishment is remedial. Behind this controversy lurks the teaching of universalism, which has it, that in the end everyone will be saved, even though the ungodly may have to go through a period of cleansing by fire, as it were. But the New Testament knows nothing about this kind of purgatory.

A question that often comes up when the topic of final judgment is under discussion, is this: How will God judge those who have never heard the gospel? The New Testament nowhere answers that directly. However, Jesus and the apostles hold out no hope for those who reject the gospel. Dr. James Packer, writing in ***Christianity Today***, says, "Our job...is to spread the gospel, not to guess what might happen to those to whom it never comes. Dealing with them is God's business; he is just, and also merciful; and when we learn, as one day we shall, how he has treated them, we shall have no cause to complain. Meantime, let us keep before our minds mankind's universal need of forgiveness and the new birth, and the graciousness of the 'whoever will' invitations in the gospel. And let us redouble our efforts to make known the Christ who saves to the uttermost all who come to God by him."

In contrast to those who are condemned by the divine Judge on the last day, are those who expressed their faith in deeds of mercy. They enter into eternal life. Eternal life is qualitatively different from biological, physical life here on earth. It is life in the age to come, life in the heavenly world. For that reason the adjective "eternal" is preferable to "everlasting," which speaks of the quantity of life. Eternal life is also everlasting, but in addition it is life on a higher plane. Believers on earth have the privilege of having a foretaste of eternal life: "Whoever believes in the Son has eternal life (Jn 3:36).

CONCLUDING OBSERVATIONS

It should be remembered that parables do not tell us everything; they have basically one major thrust, although subordinate truths are also touched upon. Nothing is said in this parable about Christ's atoning death, the forgiveness of sins, justification by faith, and so forth. Here the final judgment of humanity is in focus. We have other passages in the New Testament that make a distinction between the judgment of the believers and that of the unbelievers. Such passages do not contradict each other, but give us a fuller picture of the final judgment.

The Judge in this parable doesn't ask people when they were saved; he looks only at the fruit of that experience. "You see then that a person is justified by works, and not by faith alone," writes James (2:18). We can understand why Martin Luther had little use for the epistle of James, and in his German Bible that letter stands as far back as he could push it. For him Paul's doctrine of justification by faith was the central message of the gospel. But Luther's beloved Paul was in full harmony with James. Both agree that a genuine faith expresses itself in deeds of mercy.

Lord Shaftsbury, a famous British philanthropist, had spent both his fortune and his energy in helping the poor and the downtrodden. When he died in 1885, and the funeral cortege passed into Parliament Street, there was an unforgettable scene. Grouped on either side of the street were deputations from homes and asylums and schools and societies and missions and charities he had helped to sponsor. Each of these groups carried a banner hung with crepe. And on each banner were emblazoned the words of Jesus from our parable: "I was hungry and you gave me to eat; I was thirsty and you gave me to drink; I was a stranger and you took me in; I was naked and you clothed me; I was sick and you visited me; I was in prison and you came to me." Jesus said, "What you did to the least of these my brothers, you did it unto me."

Other Books by David Ewert

How the Bible Came to Us
Stalwart for the Truth
Die Wunderwege Gottes mit der Gemeinde
And Then Comes the End (in Spanish and Portuguese)
The Holy Spirit in the New Testament
From Ancient Tablets to Modern Translations
The Church In a Pagan Society
Proclaim Salvation
A Journey of Faith
When the Church was Young
A Testament of Joy
The Church Under Fire
Honor These People
Ist das Heil verlierbar?
Dec Heilige Geist—sein Wesen und Wirken
Verstehst du was du liesest?
How to Understand the Bible
Finding Our Way
Searching the Scriptures
Emmanuel: God Is With Us
Mark's Passion Narrative
The Body of Christ, the Church
The Church, the New People of God
Mennonite Country Boy
In the Beginning Was the Word

ABOUT THE AUTHOR

David Ewert has been involved in the teaching and preaching ministry at home and abroad since 1944. After attending several Bible training schools, he earned degrees from The University of British Columbia (B.A.), Wheaton Graduate School (M.A.), Central Baptist Seminary, Toronto (B.D.), Luther Seminary (M.Th.), and McGill University, Montreal (Ph.D.).

He was recently awarded an honorary doctorate by the Mennonite Brethren Biblical Seminary, Fresno, California.

David is the author of numerous articles and books in the field of biblical studies. He and his wife are the parents of five children, twelve grandchildren, and two great-grandchildren. David and Lena presently make their home in Abbotsford, BC. They are members of the Bakerview Mennonite Brethren Church.

www.ingramcontent.com/pod-product-compliance
Lightning Source LLC
Chambersburg PA
CBHW070640050426
42451CB00008B/236